Molly Meacher

Scrounging on the Welfare
The Scandal of the 4 Week Rule

Arrow Books

To Michael

Arrow Books Ltd
3 Fitzroy Square, London W1

London Melbourne Sydney Auckland
Wellington Johannesburg Cape Town
and agencies throughout the world

First published in Arrow Books Ltd 1974
© Molly Meacher 1974
Diagrams © Arrow Books Ltd 1974

Set in Monotype Times
Printed in Great Britain by The Anchor Press Ltd
and bound by Wm Brendon & Son Ltd
both of Tiptree, Essex

ISBN 0 09 909880 6

Contents

1 Jo 9

2 Abuse by whom? 14

3 How the four week rule works 33

4 Morality, motivation and the Welfare State 42

5 The effects of loosely worded rules 60

6 Staff problems and the communication gap 86

7 The national implications 104

8 Conclusions and recommendations 106

  Postscript 116

  Appendices 117

Acknowledgements

This study involved a nationwide survey requiring contacts with 7074 individuals in twenty-five different areas in the country. My thanks to the Leverhulme Trust Fund whose generous grant made possible a study of sufficient dimensions to provide meaningful information about some of Britain's most controversial citizens, and the effects of their experiences with the Supplementary Benefits Commission.

I am indebted to the Social and Community Planning Research and particularly to Miss Jean Morton-Williams who supervised the field-work for the study and whose scientific approach to her work adds weight to the controversial results of the survey.

Thank you, Francis Bennett of Hutchinsons, for your good humour throughout the publication process despite the difficulties encountered.

And finally a sincere thank you must be said to the people whose feelings, attitudes and experiences are described in the following pages. People who must necessarily remain anonymous, but whose experiences were, I hope, suffered to some effect.

M.M.

1 Jo

Government's anti-scrounger policy in action

Jo is tall and thin with short hair and wears a clean though well-worn anorak and pair of jeans. He is highly intelligent with eight 'O' and 'A' level passes to his credit and at the age of eighteen might be expected to have the world at his feet. A skin infection, however, has transformed the life-style of this young man from a comfortable existence at home with his parents and a steady job through a series of events, beginning with his claim for supplementary benefit, to his final downfall, remand in custody for burglary, and commitment to a mental hospital for six months.

As a baker Jo got on well with his fellow workers, found the work satisfying and regarded the money as good (£22 per week in 1971). But within six months at the job, he developed dermatitis and was told by the factory doctor to leave. The social security officer, to whom he applied for benefit while he searched for another job, insisted that he had left his work voluntarily and so refused to grant him any benefit until an investigation had been carried out. This took almost six weeks, after which Jo's youth unemployment pay of £3·10p was augmented by £2 per week. During this period Jo was still living with his parents, so the situation was not desperate.

Under a new rule introduced in July 1968 a single unskilled man under the age of forty-five is granted Supplementary Benefit for only four weeks in areas where the Employment Exchange is of the opinion that unskilled work is available. Jo's supplementary benefit of £2 per week was, however, granted for a mere three weeks (under a regulation commonly referred to as the four week rule), after which he received only his unemployment pay of £3·10p. It was assumed by the authorities that Jo could find work, but in the West Midlands in July 1971 the rate of unemployment was 3·8 per cent (higher than the rate of unemployment in Scotland and Wales in 1969 when both areas were excluded from the operation of the four week rule on the grounds that jobs were *not* readily available in these regions). Not surprisingly then the youth employment and welfare officers in the area were unable to find Jo a job, and he himself looked in vain. During the three weeks he admitted that he felt pretty low and would have taken any job offered, but despite his 'O' and 'A' levels, the level of unemployment at the time prevented him finding work of any kind.

Meanwhile his mother became increasingly impatient. His father had been retired early due to ill-health and his sister was also unable to find employment. Jo's mother threatened to evict him if he could not continue to pay £4 per week for his keep. When the supplementary benefit was withdrawn, the tension resulted in a scene and Jo felt bound to leave home – but from home to nothing. He had only £3·10p per week and yet the rents charged in the area at that time were in the region of £8 to £9 per week. The only hope was a hostel run by a religious order which required a weekly payment of £4·50.

The gap between £3·10 and £4·50 had to be met and met it was, at first by borrowing from friends and by selling scrap, but the employment situation was becoming no easier towards the end of 1971 and these methods of raising money were inadequate in the longer term. A desperate plea to the welfare officer was of no avail – 'Sorry, Jo, there's absolutely nothing I can do to help at the moment'. An offer to join a burglary seemed too good to miss at this juncture. The £50–£60 promised could solve a lot of problems. Instead Jo was remanded in custody following the burglary and soon afterwards suffered a mental breakdown which caused him to spend six months in a mental hospital. Since Jo's experiences are not uncommon and shed some light on a number of fundamental problems of any modern industrial society, he cannot be dismissed as a crank and his case forgotten.

What is the Four Week Rule to which Jo was subjected?

In July 1968 the Government introduced a 'limited awards system' which has come to be known as the four week rule. The rule stipulates that any single, unskilled man under the age of forty-five is granted supplementary benefit for only four weeks. Only under certain conditions does the rule operate however and these may be summarized as:

1. If unskilled jobs are available in the locality.

2. If the claimant is not suffering from any serious physical disability and has shown no signs of mental disorder.

3. If the claimant is unskilled.

Questions about the rule

Jo is just one of a quarter of a million men to whom the four week rule has been applied since its introduction in 1968. Many of these men were skilled, and living in areas where appropriate work was not available.

Many others have suffered or were suffering from mental illnesses at the time of their unemployment.

Still others have criminal histories and have extreme difficulty in finding regular work even in areas where work is theoretically available.

The primary objective of the four week rule is to prevent the leadswingers from living a comfortable life at the expense of the taxpayer. But Jo, for one, is no leadswinger – he emphasized his boredom and anxiety during his period of unemployment and explained that his asthma which afflicted him regularly was worse whilst he was unemployed.

The problem of handling abuse becomes apparent as soon as an individual case is examined. How, in the course of a brief interview in a crowded office, can an officer distinguish between a genuine case of need such as that described above and a man with no intention to work? In order to make a rational decision about the methods required to deal with the problem, one must have a clear picture of the extent of abuse in the field of claims for supplementary benefit in relation to abuse in other fields of activity. If supplementary benefit abuse absorbs a significant portion of revenue, then an elaborate programme of controls may be justified. If on the other hand abuse accounts for a negligible amount of Government revenue, then the social consequences of control procedures which become apparent from the brief discussion of Jo's case may constitute too high a cost to pay for the elimination of that abuse.

The extent of abuse by different sections of society including the unemployed will be examined in Chapter 2, followed by a discussion of the methods used by society to deal with the problem of abuse by the unemployed.

Why was it felt necessary in 1968 to introduce a rule depriving Jo and others like him of their benefits? Did the Government of the time believe that the powerful motivating force of the protestant ethic (the belief in the intrinsic moral value of hard work and thrift) had declined irrevocably? That young people today will not choose to work so that they must be forced to do so by means of deprivation? To what extent have men and women today lost the will to work? If the protestant ethic no longer drives men to work, then what kind of work ethic have we in its place? An attempt to answer these questions will be made in Chapter 4.

The authors of the rule clearly recognized that a number of the unskilled unemployed under the age of forty-five would be suffering from physical or mental disabilities. It is perfectly clear from the *Supplementary Benefits Handbook* HMSO (2nd ed., page 43, para. 169) that the four week rule should only apply to those who are free from any serious physical disabilities and who have shown no signs of mental disorder or instability. Discretion is required to decide whether or not a claimant is suffering from a *serious* physical disability, and furthermore to decide whether or not he has shown signs of mental instability. The official line therefore, contrary to what actually happened in Jo's case, is that a man dismissed from work on medical grounds should not have his benefit withdrawn after three weeks without a medical examination.

Discretion is also required to decide in the light of local employment conditions whether or not the rule should apply at a particular office. In view of the inability of the welfare and youth employment officers to find a job for Jo, the rule should probably not have been applied in the area at all. The general problem of the exercise of discretion is brought into question. Should any individual be deprived of this livelihood at the discretion of another individual? The inconsistencies and errors occurring; the pressure and shortage of staff and effect of public attitudes on the relationship between claimant and officer will be discussed in Chapter 5.

How far can the treatment of Jo be seen as a fault of the official concerned, or alternatively should an error of this kind be seen as an inevitable consequence of the conflict of goals of the Supplementary Benefits Commission? The problems faced by the staff will be looked at in Chapter 6 before an evaluation is made of the operation and social consequences of the four week rule in Chapter 7. Finally (in Chapter 8) the present role of the Supplementary Benefits Commission will be questioned and an alternative very different form and function proposed.

2 Abuse by whom?

'I like meeting me mates for a drink and going down the betting shop. I don't want to work at all.'

How serious is the problem of abuse of social security benefits?

The Fisher Committee reported on the extent of abuse of social security benefits in March 1973 and it is worth comparing the evidence of abuse given in that report with the evidence available of abuse by other sections of the population in order to try and put in perspective the question of abuse by supplementary benefit recipients:

Abuse of benefits—evidence available in 1973

1. In each of the three years 1969–71 surveys carried out by the Department of Health and Social Security inspectors involving more than 10 000 insured persons yielded fraud prosecutions of less than 1 per cent of claimants. (*Report of the Committee on Abuse of Social Security Benefits*, page 53, para. 158a.)

2. In surveys carried out by the Department of Health and Social Security Inspectors in 1970 covering 26 500 people including unemployed men, employers and the self employed, the total number of cases of unemployment or supplementary benefit fraud discovered was 100 (i.e. 0·4 per cent), most of it trivial (ibid. para. 158b).

3. A record kept in 1969 of overlapping contributions and credits showed that of 5210 cases of sickness and industrial injury benefit investigated, 3 per cent were considered for prosecution (ibid. para. 158c).

4. A check is kept of retirement pensioners who are earning sufficient for a contribution stamp to be paid for them, and

in 52 000 cases checked, 4·3 per cent were found to have earnings over the limit which had not been declared (ibid. para. 158d).

5. A 1971 survey found that the amount of undiscovered over-payments due to wrongful claims in sickness benefit cases (where the husband claimed for his wife as a dependent when she was working) came to about 1 per cent of the total paid for dependent wives. For unemployment benefit the extent of overpayments was 1·4 per cent. Interestingly enough, the costs of the enquiry were about eight times the amount of overpayments discovered!

6. Evidence of voluntary unemployment or, as it is popularly called, 'scrounging' is even more hard to find. The most thorough official survey of the problem ever undertaken by the National Assistance Board in 1956 found that of the 32 000 persons interviewed who had been unemployed for two years or more and were drawing national assistance, only 7 per cent were considered 'workshy' and over 3·5 of these were physically or mentally handicapped, leaving only 2·8 per cent voluntarily unemployed claimants.

One qualification

The only group of supplementary benefit recipients about whom there is any evidence at all of extensive abuse is the liable relative group (usually separated wives, unmarried mothers and some divorcees). A local study of 184 cases in the East Midlands revealed fraud in 30 per cent of cases. However, a very much larger study, of 152 000 'liable relative' cases, selected as being the most likely to be fraudulent, revealed fraud in only 7·3 per cent of cases.

Even so it is difficult to see how any objective person can conclude from this review of the evidence that 'abuse by wrongful claims is a serious problem'. Yet that was the central finding of the Fisher Committee (paragraph 488).

But are the unemployed a lot of scroungers?

When the Fisher Committee remained unconvinced by the evidence available to them, it became apparent that a closer look at the problem was necessary in order to try and establish precisely the proportion of claimants who are workshy and the reasons for any reluctance to work. It was in this context that the present study of 7074 men in the North, Midlands, South East and South West of the country was carried out. The survey included ninety-eight men to whom the four week rule had been applied and who were willing to be interviewed at some length.

The evidence of our own survey
The reasons why people remain unemployed

The main difficulties which lead to prolonged unemployment are the age and health condition of the claimants or the lack of local job opportunities. These are the findings of a 1961 study as well as of our own survey carried out in 1973 and illustrated in the following diagram. More relevant to our discussion is the very small proportion of claimants who remain unemployed 'for social reasons including attitudes to work'.

Studies in 1951, 1955, 1956, 1958 and 1960 also concluded that the hard core of the unemployed consisted to a very large

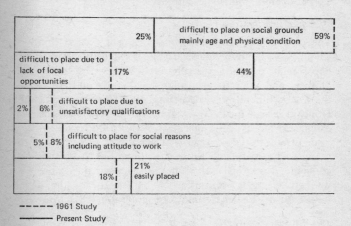

-------- 1961 Study
———— Present Study

Analysis of employment prospects. Results of 1961 study of 176,000 unemployed men, and of the present study

extent of men and women suffering from some form of physical or mental disability, and that wilful idleness accounted for lengthy unemployment in only a small number of cases.

Of the ninety-eight men included in our survey fully thirty-three suffered from physical or mental illnesses varying in severity, but all sufficiently serious to have required medical treatment. In addition, thirty-six men complained of depression or sleeplessness during the period of unemployment, and of the sixty-nine men suffering from some form of mental or physical disturbance about a quarter complained of more than one problem e.g., (1) constant pain resulting from a serious accident five years previously and a speech problem resulting from the same accident; (2) stomach trouble and boils; (3) chronic bronchitis and depression; (4) venereal disease and sleeplessness.

Only 29 per cent of the sample suffered no ill effects during their period of unemployment.

Of the three groups, mentally or physically sick, the anxious

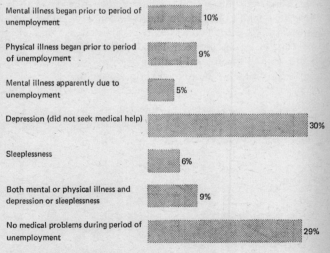

Mental illness began prior to period of unemployment — 10%

Physical illness began prior to period of unemployment — 9%

Mental illness apparently due to unemployment — 5%

Depression (did not seek medical help) — 30%

Sleeplessness — 6%

Both mental or physical illness and depression or sleeplessness — 9%

No medical problems during period of unemployment — 29%

Percentages given to nearest percentage point Total = 98%

Mental and Physical illness suffered during unemployment

or depressed and the fit, it was the members of the first group who tended to be unemployed for the longest periods. Nearly half the men (45 per cent) suffering from a mental or physical illness had been unemployed for more than six months. In contrast, only 28 per cent of the remainder of the sample had been unemployed for as long. Not surprisingly perhaps the basically fit men who complained of depression, sleeplessness or emotional disturbance during their period of unemployment were the least likely to remain unemployed for long periods. Only 19 per cent of this group were out of work for more than six months, despite the exceptionally high unemployment at the time of our interviews.

The direction of the causal link between the length of unemployment and stress symptoms might be questioned. It may be that unemployed men are likely to be particularly anxious about their situation when they have been job hunting for some three months, whereas after a period of some twelve months out of work men may fall into an apathetic or chronically depressed state of mind which might be expected to be associated with a decline in the prevalence of acute stress symptoms. All we can conclude from this study is that a clear relationship exists between length of unemployment and mental as well as physical health and stability. This relationship is illustrated in the following three graphs.

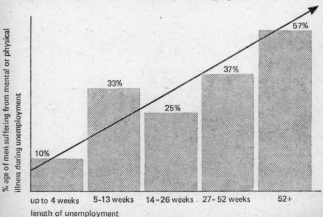

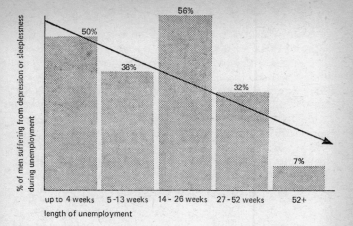

% of men suffering from depression or sleeplessness during unemployment

56%

50%

38%

32%

7%

up to 4 weeks   5 -13 weeks   14 – 26 weeks   27 - 52 weeks   52 +

length of unemployment

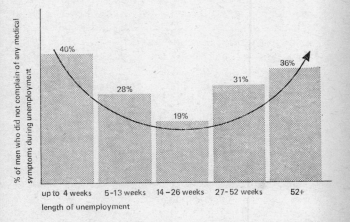

% of men who did not complain of any medical symptoms during unemployment

40%

28%

19%

31%

36%

up to 4 weeks   5 -13 weeks   14 – 26 weeks   27 - 52 weeks   52 +

length of unemployment

But the graphs also provide some information about the extent of abuse amongst the ninety-eight men interviewed.

Clearly the 33 per cent suffering from mental or physical illnesses cannot be said to be 'scrounging'.

Men suffering from sleeplessness or depression whilst un-employed (36 per cent) are unlikely to prolong the experience unnecessarily. Certainly they do not fit into the picture of men taking advantage of the dole and enjoying it on the booze.

The comments of a small number of men in the 2nd group suggested however that the despair resulting from repeated failure to secure a job led to lethargy and depression which no doubt hindered the task of job-hunting.

The group most likely to be 'voluntarily unemployed' is the third: men who have no apparent illness and who do not claim to have felt depressed or to have suffered from sleeplessness or emotional stress while unemployed (29 per cent).

It may be worth while therefore to look closely at the eleven men in this group who remained unemployed for more than six months.

1. Joc had been unemployed for seventy-two weeks and had been denied unemployment benefit and supplementary benefit for the first year. He then applied again for supplementary benefit and was granted help for five weeks only. Did he do anything more than he was already doing about finding a job when his supplementary benefit was cut?

'No', said Joc, 'I had always been looking for a job before. I couldn't do any more about it.'

He had applied for eight jobs that he could remember and also for a Government training scheme for car mechanics. However, he remained unemployed and had to wait for twelve months for a place on the training scheme. Meanwhile he was studying at night school doing a car maintenance course and hoped to get a job in a garage in the near future.

A significant comment suggesting that Joc was by no means 'workshy' – 'I would like to be a qualified skilled mechanic – there are usually jobs available for that'.

A casual observer or inquisitive neighbour might well suggest that such a person is 'workshy' but the facts suggest that here is a man determined to work his way into a skilled and reliable job.

2. Dave may indeed be a scrounger (ready to accept State help when he could manage without it), but he is far from 'workshy'. He works long hours as a pop artist touring the country and travelling abroad but all the proceeds from performances are either invested in equipment and are

used to meet the costs of promoting the group. Dave was receiving £4 a week allowance from his parents (his father was a company director), and admitted that he did not apply for social security out of necessity.

Dave is one of the very few men interviewed for this study who might justifiably have been denied benefit from the outset. He had no food or lodging expenses and had a small private income and an exciting job. And yet although Dave was threatened with the four week rule, his benefit continued to be paid without any re-application. It is hard to find any justification for this decision, particularly in the light of so many adverse decisions against men in very real need.

3. John lives with his parents and had paid sufficient stamps to qualify him for £3·32p per week unemployment benefit – his only income – when his supplementary benefit was cut after four weeks. John claims that he combed the local factories for jobs but it was hopeless – in one case twelve people went along for the same job. He disliked being unemployed and was taking a twelve month course in car body work after which he hopes to emigrate to Australia and get a good job. 'Workshy'? Anything but that. A scrounger? Yes, but a reluctant one and the sufferer is his mother, not the State.

4. Harold lived on baked beans and Ricicles when his benefit was withdrawn, except for one evening when he enjoyed the luxury of some stolen fish. He disliked being unemployed and finally opted for a less skilled and lower paid job than he had had prior to his period of unemployment. At the time of the interview he was employed as an unskilled labourer in a timber yard and planned either to stay there or to emigrate to Canada to work in the timber industry. *One of the unexpected findings of the survey has been the very high proportion of respondents, fully 20 per cent, who mentioned plans to go abroad.* This perhaps reflects a deep dissatisfaction with employment prospects in this country.

5. Jack, aged twenty, had already done three years of a full five-year car mechanics apprenticeship and wanted to do the

last two years. However, having been dismissed for poor timekeeping by his previous employer, Jack had no idea how to set about applying to do the remainder of his course, or whether, in fact, he could do the two years without paying the fees himself. He complained bitterly that the employment exchange didn't give him any helpful advice or information.

Jack asserted: 'I'm a mechanic. I love doing repairs to cars.' But after six months searching for an appropriate job he accepted a less skilled labouring post. He resented the tedium of the work and claimed that he would rather be paid less and be a mechanic than do the work he was doing.

6. Larry is the sixth member of the long-term fit unemployed who, I feel confident in saying, is not workshy. He is a Jamaican who has struggled against the odds to find work in a situation of peak unemployment, but had reached the point at the time of our interview of hoping to return to Jamaica. Up to that time he had been able to meet the cost of his rent from his own savings, but was becoming increasingly desperate having been without any State help or a job for more than a year.

7. Bill had been unemployed for about a year, though he claimed that he would prefer to be in work all the time. In addition to the lack of job opportunities at the time, Bill's employment prospects were further reduced due to his dependence on his mother and his reluctance to work even two miles away from home. His employment record was unimpressive. After taking two Fridays off work in his previous job and despite a warning, Bill persisted in remaining at home on Fridays and duly received his cards. Bill had resigned from the job before that because 'they messed me about too much'. The field was therefore narrowed both geographically and by building up an unfavourable reputation in the local firms.

On the surface, Bill would seem to have mild personality problems, and in order to decide an appropriate course of action, a careful investigation would be needed by the Supplementary Benefits Commission, instead of which the four week rule was applied automatically after the usual visit to enable financial details to be checked. Bill is an obvious candidate for neighbours who wish to nail their resentments on an apparent loafer, but it seems doubtful that any such allegations would be supported by a deeper investigation.

8. Fred, on the other hand, is a professional thief of some sixteen years experience, seven of which have been spent behind bars. 'Workshy'? Only in society's terms, not according to his own definitions. Scrounger? Good Heavens no! What use is £4 to anyone! Of course if the State will give him a bit of money, he'll be quite happy to take it, but he will continue to work hard at his 'profession' where he believes the real money lies. 'If I wanted £20 a week I could work, but I want to retire at forty-five with a house of my own, so the only "jobs" I go for are worth at least £150.'

Fred began on the straight and narrow road down the pits when he left school for a paltry wage of £12 per week. He claims it was that experience which made him what he is.

'Why should I work for someone to make a profit out of me?' he asks, and one sees what he means. Perhaps the surprising thing about Fred's attitude is the fact that so few unskilled men apparently share it. Why should any individual work long, uncomfortable and often dangerous hours every day of his working life while others reap the profits and spend their afternoons golfing after an unnecessarily luxurious business lunch?

Fred's response to the withdrawal of his benefit was to go out thieving for £500. It seems clear that no action by the social security officials would have any effect on Fred's activities.

A solution to the problem of individuals like Fred is beyond the scope of this study, but a more constructive approach than the removal of benefit might be the provision of an appropriate training course for satisfying and financially rewarding work.

9. Ben is an unhappy nineteen-year-old, his girl friend is pregnant, and he feels unduly heavily punished for thieving. He

takes the view, not unjustifiably, that the prison sentence should be his only punishment, whereas in fact he also loses his entitlement to unemployment benefit, is threatened by the Supplementary Benefits Commission with the withdrawal of his benefit, and finds it particularly hard to find a job.

Ben is keen to work and takes the line that he must do something 'especially now my girl friend is going to have a baby, but there is just nothing to be had round here'. Of his previous job as machine operator he commented: 'I was very satisfied – well, I was happy to be going to work.' However he was in trouble with the police and his prison sentence brought his job to an end. He admits to a bad temper which leads him to fight easily. Furthermore he readily admits that he did break-ins on the way home from his girl friend in the evenings when he got the chance.

Ben reapplied successfully for his supplementary benefit when it was cut after four weeks. One suspects that if the full facts of Ben's circumstances were known, he would lose all entitlement to benefit and yet the withdrawal of help could, on Ben's own admission, lead to more serious crimes and would almost certainly, therefore, be unwise.

10. Bert was unemployed for the first half of 1972 – a time of peak unemployment exaggerated by the miners' strike in February of that year. Bert was able to find a few casual jobs during this six month period. He used the proceeds of these jobs to supplement his benefit and was therefore in official terms abusing the Supplementary Benefits Commission, and would no doubt be referred to by his neighbours as a scrounger. However when asked whether he was satisfied with the job he had before becoming unemployed he replied: 'Yes I was satisfied to have a job and some money.' This is not the response of a man who enjoys drawing State benefits.

Bert had never known his father, and his mother was dead. (He was twenty-seven at the time of the interview and we do not know how long ago he had lost his mother.) He had been in trouble with the police on several occasions, the first being at the age of sixteen. He had been committed to Borstal on two occasions and had served two three-year sentences in prison. At the time of our interview Bert had lost his job as a result of an illness and had therefore begun his twelfth period of unemployment since he left school. He was luckier than many in that he lived with his uncle and aunt and had the security of a home. But nevertheless Bert was a lonely and aimless figure who, without any qualifications or skills, and a criminal record, was inevitably one of the first to lose out in a period of depression.

11. Harry, on the other hand, had a very clear idea of what he wanted to do. The central reason for his prolonged unemployment was his lack of the necessary qualifications to do the job he had in mind. He thought in terms of being a television engineer and applied for jobs in this field on the assumption that he could soon learn all he needed to know. Not surprisingly he had failed to secure a job and had finally, after nine months out of work, applied for a Government Training Scheme for television engineers. Despite Harry's claim that he felt everyone should have six months' holiday after five years' work 'like Directors do', he appeared quite happy to work on condition that the job was the one he wanted and that it would provide adequate pay.

He would not consider taking 'any old job, just for the money'. He was one of the few individuals for whom the protestant ethic meant very little.

The workshy – who are they?

We have felt it worthwhile to spend some time repeating the comments and circumstances of the eleven fit long term unemployed men in order to make as clear as possible the evidence behind my conclusion from this study that probably only one of the long-term unemployed men in our sample could be termed a scrounger – our professional thief. Only he showed a willingness to draw benefit without any intention of taking a steady job and with no intention of declaring his financial position. His moral values diverged markedly from those of the remainder of the sample, and indeed from society at large. Two others, Bert and Harry, might be regarded by some as belonging to the same category, but they do not fall within my definition of a scrounger: an individual with no mental or physical disability, who would prefer to remain unemployed rather than to take an official job of the kind to which they are accustomed or for which they have been trained. Bert expressed his satisfaction to be working and Harry had applied for a training course at the time of our interview.

One other claimant, Pete, could be included within the definition of a scrounger. He had been unemployed for only fourteen weeks at the time of our interview and was therefore not discussed at length in the preceding paragraphs. But he explained that he would prefer not to work if he could manage it. 'I like meeting me mates for a drink and going down the betting shop. I don't want to work at all.'

Although Pete did not admit to doing any thieving the interviewer said she felt that he supplemented his winnings in the betting shop with a few 'jobs' on the side. He certainly differed from our professional thief, Fred, who took a pride in his 'profession'. In fact Pete seemed ambivalent about the merits of an idle life. He had been a skilled upholsterer for about four years and said he was very satisfied with the job. He had earned £50 a week, liked the 'fellers' and was never told what to do – 'you just carried on yourself like' he explained with obvious satisfaction. As business slackened in early 1972, however, five of the seven skilled men were made redundant including Pete. After fourteen weeks of unemployment he had no wish to return to work. He did not reclaim benefit after the four week period because he didn't want to spend 'another four hours' sitting in the office. He considered that for £4 the wait was too long. He explained that he had never before claimed benefit of any sort so that despite his willingness to remain idle he was not a burden to the State purse, and was not positively affected by the four week rule. The meagre £4 per week did not deter him from work and its withdrawal did not drive him to work either.

The findings of this study bring into question the view so

often expressed that the welfare state is supporting a growing army of scroungers or young people who have no wish to work.

If the definition of 'the workshy' already quoted is accepted, then Fred and Pete are the only two claimants of the ninety-eight interviewed to whom the definition could apply. We might therefore conclude very tentatively that some 2 per cent or so of all four week rule claimants are likely to be similarly workshy.

If this gives some idea of the extent of fraudulent claims of social security, especially the relatively meagre sums involved, what of the extent of abuse elsewhere in society?

Tax fraud

In the decade 1963–72 fully £93 907 232 of taxes were re-claimed by the Exchequer from just over one hundred thousand persons after it had been revealed that they had illegally evaded full payment of their taxes (Table 25, *Report of the Commissioners of H.M. Inland Revenue* for the year ended 31.1.72). Also £10¼m tax liabilities have been annually remitted or written off as irrecoverable, 87 per cent of which were income tax and surtax dues. In almost half the cases the taxpayer had 'gone abroad or was untraceable'. These figures are to be compared with the evidence of overpayments of supplementary benefit due to fraud – £304 000 in 1972, the first year for which this information is available. If we assume that in every one of the past ten years the level of overpayments were at this level, then in contrast to nearly £94m of reclaimed taxes, a mere £3m was overpaid to supplementary benefit recipients due to fraud.

Just one example of one rule for the rich and another for the poor is that of the Recorder, Mr Norman Fox Andrews, QC. After investigation by the Inland Revenue's Inquiry Branch in 1965 he was found to have cheated the Exchequer of 'several thousands of pounds in unpaid taxes', but though criminal proceedings were recommended by the Solicitors' Branch, this was overruled by the Board of the Inland Revenue on the grounds that 'prosecution would undermine public

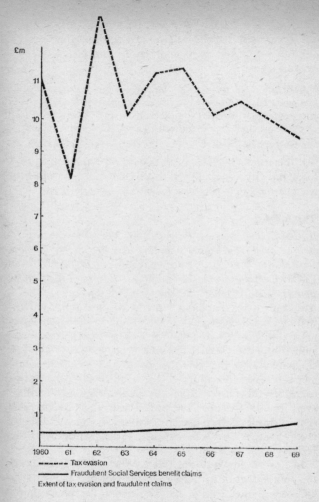

£m

11 —
10 —
9 —
8 —
7 —
6 —
5 —
4 —
3 —
2 —
1 —

1960 61 62 63 64 65 66 67 68 69

- - - - Tax evasion
——— Fraudulent Social Services benefit claims

Extent of tax evasion and fraudulent claims

Sources: top graph calculated from Table 25, 112th report of Commissioners of Inland Revenue, Jan. 1970, Comnd. 4262. Bottom graph calculated from Hansard, 13th April, 1970, written answers, Col. 162, together with Accounts of National Insurance Fund, 1959–1960 to 1968–69.

The difference in treatment of tax defrauders as against benefit defrauders (1972)

Tax Defrauders	Benefit Defrauders
£9m of taxes to the Inland Revenue were proved to have been illegally evaded and not paid.	£0·3m of supplementary benefit was overpaid to claimants due to fraud.
The average sum involved, excluding penalties, was nearly £1000 in each individual case.	The average sum involved, excluding penalties, was £21 in each individual case.
Only 1 per cent of these persons were prosecuted.	Fully 40 per cent of fraudulent claimants were prosecuted in 1972. Of these,
	6 per cent were imprisoned
	8 per cent received a suspended sentence
	65 per cent were fined
	19 per cent received 'other penalties'
	2 per cent were acquitted.

confidence' (*Guardian*, 17.12.73). One might well argue that the revelation of official connivance at these irregularities undermines public confidence much more. This is particularly so when the Treasury recently revealed, in answer to a Parliamentary Question, that in 1972–73 there were 250 cases where profits were admitted, after Revenue investigations, to have been under-declared by £10 000 or more; yet there were only 17 prosecutions for false accounts and fraudulent returns of income, while 80 000 cases were settled quietly behind the scenes. *Unofficial estimates by Inland Revenue staff of the present scale of (illegal) evasion range as high as £1000 millions or 10 per cent of the total tax collected.*

No figures are available for the hundreds of millions lost to the Exchequer in death duties by the setting up of discretionary trusts and the use of other loopholes. One outlandish device is the 45 per cent reduction of estate duty at a stroke by the (literally) death bed purchase of agricultural property or woodlands. This form of tax avoidance is reflected in the

Forestry Commission's census of private woodlands which showed in 1965 that over 2 500 000 acres of woodland, possibly worth £500m, was owned privately – a figure more than 50 per cent greater than land in public ownership.

It is not officially known how many private discretionary and other family settlements (which are not subject to death duties) are at present in operation in Britain, nor the amount of capital thus tied up, though it must total several hundred million pounds. However, one of the tax advisers to the Conservative Party, Professor Wheatcroft, has stated that 95 per cent of all discretionary and accumulation trusts are created solely for tax saving reasons. Other forms of tax avoidance are covenants taken out in favour of grand-children; certain forms of life assurance under the Married Women's Property Act 1882; accumulation settlements in favour of infants; and covenants for separation agreements and divorce orders. The loss to the Exchequer from these devices is unknown, but is undoubtedly enormous.

Tax havens

Finally, the use of tax havens such as the Channel Islands, the Isle of Man, and Gibraltar, not only by wealthy individuals but also by giant international companies and merchant banks amongst others, must cost hundreds of millions of pounds to the Exchequer each year. Funds deposited with the Channel Islands have grown unprecedentedly since the winding up of the Sterling area. In Jersey more than 1000 new companies were set up in 1972 compared with 430 in 1971, and funds deposited probably total more than £800m. As a result of such contrivances B.P., for instance, in which the Government are a 49 per cent shareholder, pays no tax whatsoever to the British Exchequer, though a third of its workers work in this country.

The official lack of knowledge of the extent of tax avoidance (legal, but anti-social) and evasion (illegal), and the refusal to include this costly area of abuse within the scope of the Fisher Committee, established to examine the abuse of social security benefits, was highly significant. Why, one wonders, when it was known that very much larger sums of money were involved in the tax abuse field, did the Treasury only establish a sub-committee of the Tax Reform Committee privately within the Inland Revenue to report to the Chancellor 'in confidence from time to time' on the anti-tax avoidance provisions generally?

The conniving attitude of the (then) British Government towards tax avoidance was revealed by its tacit approval of the development of a new tax haven in the Pacific, the otherwise unheard-of New Hebrides, at the very time (May 1973) that the Lonrho tax avoidance scandals were revealed. The Islands' largest trust company claimed (*Guardian*, 13.5.73) that 'the British Administration moved in quickly to regulate, without discouraging, the orderly development of Vila (the capital) as a financial centre'. Furthermore, the EEC itself was brazen enough to give its official approval to the Channel Islands and the Isle of Man as tax havens. These islands have been free to benefit from the customs union and free trade provisions of the Treaty of Rome, but have not been obliged to harmonize their tax systems.

With the return of a Labour Government in March 1974 a start has been made towards tackling the problem of tax avoidance and evasion. After only three weeks in office Denis Healey eliminated the possibility of using tax havens in the way described above by taxing 90 per cent of all foreign based earnings whether or not the money is remitted to the United Kingdom. Secondly the Chancellor stipulated that children's investment income will once again be added to parents' income for tax purposes so that payment of tax cannot be avoided by putting money in a child's name, and then regarding the two incomes as separate when declaring them to the Inland Revenue authorities. Perhaps at least as important as either of these reforms in the long run will be the new Gifts Tax with which the 1974 Government plans to replace Estate Duty.

Nevertheless these measures were, as the Chancellor admitted at the time, only a beginning. What is undoubtedly still needed is an unfettered public inquiry into the full extent of tax avoidance and secret 'deals' in Britain today. This would need to be followed by a comprehensive tax avoidance statute which should enable the Revenue to enforce the spirit of the legislature's intentions.

'Fringe benefits' and other abuse

At least 8–10 per cent of British Rail underground receipts are lost each year due to fare evasion, according to the Chairman of London Transport (letter from Chairman 14.4.72). In money terms the loss amounts to at least £5m, a sum which is paid in the long run by the 90 per cent or so of honest passengers.

One last area of abuse is that which is curiously entitled 'fringe benefits'. They are anything but fringe. They include 'top hat' private pension schemes. Are all these 'fringe' benefits and tax avoidance manoeuvres less worthy of investigation and control than the young lad who picks up £5 a week supplementary benefit, and does some work on a building site when he gets a chance, while looking for a steady job?

The cost of abuses

Abuse is therefore by no means confined to people living at or below the poverty level. In a materialistic society, where the competitive pursuit of financial gain is paramount, it is inevitable that abuse of the public interest persists at every income level. *The important point however which this survey of the facts has demonstrated is that the extent of the abuse and the cost to the public purse is far greater the more financial power and opportunities people have, particularly at the top.*

3 How the Four Week Rule Works

It has, I hope, been established that the cost of the 'scrounger' drawing supplementary benefit is very small when compared to the cost of various forms of tax evasion and tax avoidance. I will now go on to outline the procedures to control abuse by claimants already in operation before the four week rule was introduced in 1968, to summarize the extension of controls which make up the four week rule and to try and justify the administrative machinery in the light of the very limited extent of the problem concerned.

According to the Ministry of Social Security Act 1966, every person in Great Britain of or over the age of sixteen whose resources are insufficient to meet his requirements is entitled to a supplementary benefit. But this right is subject to several stringent conditions which we now outline.

What happens when you make a claim?

First visit to the social security office

If an appointments system is organized then a claimant may be called for an interview after waiting for only a short time (but unlucky claimants have been known to wait for up to four hours to be interviewed).

At this first interview the officer will try to establish that all the necessary conditions are fulfilled by the claimant. These include:

(a) that the claimant is out of work *through no fault of his own;*

(b) that he has not refused suitable employment without good reason;

(c) that his total income in the relevant week is in fact below the specified level of requirements;

(d) that his wife is not earning more than the statutory £2;

(e) that his capital is sufficiently small not to disqualify him from benefit.

Checking documents

In order to establish that all the above conditions apply, the Commission has the power under Regulation 4 of the Supplementary Benefits (Claims and Payments) Regulations 1966 to require 'such certificates, documents, information and evidence for the purpose of determining the claim as may be required'.

Further investigations and home visit

If the official is not completely satisfied after one visit to the office that all the details of the claimant's statement are correct, then he will not normally make any payments until he has made a full investigation. This generally includes a visit to the home of the claimant.

If a claimant explains that his need is urgent, however, then a small payment may be made after one visit to the office even if a few details remain to be checked.

During a home visit the rent book, rate demand forms, mortgage documents, pay slips, pension order books, etc., will be checked and if necessary the bank manager will be contacted. More significant though is the automatic check on the employment situation which a home visit involves. If either or both the claimant and his wife are out, then enquiries will be made to ensure that neither are working. In one case recorded in a recent survey, for instance, both parents were out and a child opened the door to a Supplementary Benefit Officer who asked where the child's father was. The child did not know, but assumed his father was at work and said so. Needless to say no benefit was paid to the family concerned, despite the fact that the father was not at work at all, but was in fact looking for a job.

There are four main methods of control in addition to the four week rule which are designed to prevent abuse of the supplementary benefit scheme.

1. Immediate refusal or withdrawal of supplementary benefit

If, according to an official from the employment exchange, a person has been discharged from work for misconduct, or if he left voluntarily without good reason, or has refused suitable employment without good reason, then if no appeal is outstanding, supplementary benefit may be refused or withdrawn if the following conditions are fulfilled:

(a) if a specific suitable job is available to the claimant, taking into account any handicaps from which he may suffer, or;

(b) all the following conditions are satisfied and the action is authorized by a Higher Executive Officer,

   (i) there have been at least three incidents of voluntary unemployment in the last six months;

  (ii) the area is one in which job opportunities in employment suitable for the claimant are abundant and the employment exchange confirms that, in the individual case, the claimant could obtain work in his occupation without difficulty;

 (iii) the claimant is free from any mental disability;

 (iv) the claimant is free from any serious physical disability, unless exceptionally it has been agreed by the Disablement Resettlement Officer that it would be in the man's best interest to withdraw the allowance;

  (v) the claimant has no dependent children or, if married without children, the wife has been seen, is in good health and is herself under forty, fit for work and likely to obtain it;

 (vi) the claimant has no social handicap which would make it particularly difficult for him to find work;

(vii) there are no dependants or other persons, e.g. relatives dependent on supplementary benefit or retirement pensions or sickness benefit, in the applicant's household who might suffer hardship if an allowance were refused or withdrawn.

The conditions for withdrawal of benefit appear stringent at first glance, but their stringency depends largely upon the time available to the staff to check that all conditions are in fact satisfied. The importance of staff time will again become apparent when we turn to the four week rule itself.

The working of the rule in practice

Often the threat of withdrawal of benefit is sufficient to drive men back to work. An example of the use of the threat is that of a thirty-six year old man with homosexual tendencies and poor health whose effeminate behaviour, the officials decided, was no bar to his getting a job, and it was his idea of the work he really wanted that was a problem. The person in question wanted a job as a copywriter, but had been in and out of work for three years. He was found a job sweeping up in a packing shop for 11 gns. a week (in 1968). He turned down the job, but was warned by the Commission Officers that this would not be allowed to continue. Not long afterwards he accepted work in a factory. The question immediately arises as to whether or not a man should be expected to accept work in a factory or sweeping floors if he is qualified to do a white-collar job. The fact is however that before the four week rule was introduced the machinery existed to prevent men drawing supplementary benefit if work of almost any sort was available within a radius of about 100 miles. Officials varied in their interpretations of the concept of 'suitable employment', but if it was felt that a claimant was workshy then the wording of the relevant Acts was sufficiently vague to enable the necessary action to be taken to drive a man into work.

The laws which allow benefit to be withdrawn

The reduction or withdrawal of benefit was first allowed for in the National Assistance (Determination of Need) Regulations in 1948 which said:

'Where there are special circumstances, the amount calculated in accordance with the last foregoing regulation may be adjusted as may be appropriate to meet these circumstances'.

and again in Schedule 2 of the Ministry of Social Security Act 1966 which said:

'Where there are exceptional circumstances a Supplementary Allowance may be reduced below the amount so calculated or may be withheld as may be appropriate to take account of these circumstances'.

The principle behind these two declarations was quite different from that of the four week rule in that before 1968 benefit could *only be withdrawn in special circumstances*, whereas the four week rule involves the withdrawal of benefit after four weeks *unless there are special circumstances*.

2. The work of Unemployment Review Officers

Since 1961, when Unemployment Review Officers were introduced experimentally, the case papers of all unemployed persons who remain in DHSS files are reviewed at regular intervals by a review officer. If a claimant continues to be unemployed for no apparent reason for more than three months in an area of high employment, or for rather longer in a place where jobs are few, his case is taken over by a review officer whose job it is to discover whether there are underlying causes, such as hidden or unsuspected mental or physical handicap, domestic trouble, social maladjustment or other such factors which might explain the persisting unemployment.

This highly responsible and difficult work was done by officers with no official training (merely on-the-job experience) until 1970, since when a short training has been available.

It was revealed by Mrs Hart in a letter to the *New Statesman* in 1968, that half the claimants interviewed by a special officer (untrained in psychiatry) in an experiment with control procedures were unable to be placed in employment because they were mentally disturbed, physically limited or psychologically maladjusted. *How accurate are the assessments of untrained men of the mental fitness of the men they interview? In view of the high incidence of mental illness amongst the longer term unemployed, this question is of considerable importance.*

3. Benefit may be paid only if a claimant attends a course or lives in a special centre

Section 12 (i) of the Ministry of Social Security Act 1966 provides that a person who refuses to maintain himself or any other persons he is liable to maintain may be reported to the appeal tribunal who may direct that the payment of benefit may be conditional on:

(a) attendance at an approved course of training (Section 12/2)

(b) attendance at a residential establishment centre (Section 12/3) (these centres are being reserved for the long-term unemployed who, it is felt, may have lost the habit of work)

(c) attendance at a centre run by another Government Department or voluntary organization, but similar to a re-establishment centre (Section 12/4).

In 1971 the Supplementary Benefits Commission reported 153 cases to a Tribunal under Section 12/1 and 150 were judged to be appropriate for the conditional payment of benefit.

4. A claimant may be taken to court

If, as a result of the normal unemployment review proceedings, it is decided that a man is quite fit and has no serious domestic troubles, but is felt to be simply unwilling to work, then the Executive Officer, after a discussion with the Manager, may prepare the case for prosecution (in accordance with Section 30 of the Ministry of Social Security Act 1966). The Manager then sends the case papers to the Regional office where the agreement of the Senior Medical Officer has to be given before the case is sent to Headquarters. At Headquarters the whole history is fully examined before the decision to prosecute is finally taken by a Senior Officer. In 1971, 5753 persons were prosecuted for supplementary benefit offences, of whom 64 were accused of voluntary unemployment.

All these controls were already in existence when Judith Hart felt compelled to stiffen and extend the hurdles for the workshy in July 1968. The control procedures outlined above continue in operation alongside the four week rule, which is summarized below and explained in full in Appendix 1.

Summary of the four week rule

1. A claimant under the age of forty-five who is physically and mentally fit and who is unmarried and unskilled will be given supplementary benefit for four weeks only when he first makes a claim. If at the end of the four weeks he is still unemployed through no fault of his own then his allowance will be continued (if the rule is applied correctly).

2. After three months of unemployment the four week rule is applied to:

all married men under the age of forty-five   if they are
all skilled men under the age of forty-five   mentally and
all women under the age of forty-five   physically fit.

3. People who are not fully fit and those over the age of forty-five have their allowances reviewed after six months (or in the case of those of age sixty allowances are reviewed after about a year). The unemployment review 'specialists' are brought in for this work.

The difference between theory and practice

The operation of the four week rule is very different in practice from the careful administration suggested in the Supplementary Benefits Handbook which is, it should be noted, written for claimants, even if not often seen or read by them. In order to understand the apparently indiscriminate use of the rule against skilled men, often men with mental and physical handicaps and men with dependents who suffer bitterly when benefit is withdrawn, the staffing problems of the Supplementary Benefits Commission need to be understood and also the intentions of the Ministry which appear to diverge from the gentle tones of the Handbook. These issues will be discussed in Chapter 6, but at this point it is worth considering why a Labour Minister felt impelled to introduce the four week rule when a study of 1900 claims carried out at her request had just shown, according to the Minister herself, that only 'a very small minority' of claimants were workshy. (It is worth recalling that sources already quoted show that 0·04 per cent of supplementary benefit expenditure is wrongly paid out, compared with 8–10 per cent fraud in the case of underground fare evasion.)

Why have a four week rule at all?

The introduction of the 'rule' must be seen as a response to public resentment following the considerable publicity towards the end of 1967 in the press and on television about a few individual cases of young men apparently living on supplementary benefit and making no attempt to find work. The case for the rule rests on the undesirability of leaving young men without dependants to settle down to a life on the dole at the State's expense. The image is redolent of the hippy phenomenon – of bearded scruffy youths sleeping rough or leading promiscuous and lazy lives whilst challenging the values of their neighbours whose taxes they readily accept in the form of benefits. Not that it was known in 1968 or even now even approximately how many such 'drop-outs' exist or whether their numbers are increasing significantly. A disproportionate degree of resentment is generated by one such case on an estate, and still more by one such individual interviewed on the television. The results of adverse publicity were confirmed by an article in the *Financial Times* (David Watt, Criticism of the Welfare State, 20.9.68) which said 'It is a long time since there has been so much feeling (against those receiving social security benefits), if indeed there has ever been so much'.

The findings of a survey of attitudes to the social services carried out by Dr Mark Abrams' Research Services in 1967 showed that just over half the population believed that the Government was spending too much on the social services, and particularly on benefit for the unemployed. One of the chief objections to benefit for the unemployed was that it was too easy to draw and that there were 'too many loafers and lead swingers'. (See Appendix 2 for the only piece of evidence to support this view.)

Why is it that so much ill-feeling was and still is generated by one apparently workshy neighbour. Can the explanation lie in the real or feared decline of the the will to work? Are the critics of the unemployed *themselves* increasingly attracted by the idea of ceasing to work and drawing benefits? Is their anger really an expression of jealousy of a situation they would like for themselves? Or is their anger an expression of frustration that the life of a 'decent upright worker' has been improving all too slowly for all too long? These questions will be examined in the next chapter.

4 Morality, Motivation and the Welfare State

'The moral fibre of our people has been weakened. A state which does for its citizens what they can do for themselves is an evil state; and a state which removes all choice and responsibility from its people and makes them like broiler hens will create the irresponsible society. In such an irresponsible society no-one saves, no-one bothers – why should they when the state spends all its energies taking money from the energetic, successful and thrifty to give to the idle, the failures and the feckless?' (**Dr Rhodes Boyson**, *Down with the Poor*, Churchill Press Ltd.: 1971)

The view that state support for the elderly, the sick and the unemployed in some way weakens the moral fibre of society is shared by people in every walk of life. The following paragraphs will seek to throw some light on the question of how far people are ready to sit back and allow the state to care for their needs.

A general discussion of the qualitative changes in the morality of society will be followed by a discussion of the changing attitudes to work in particular and the influence of a freer educational curriculum on the expectation of school leavers, the effects of the welfare state on incentives to work: the problem of absenteeism and the 'drop-out' will be examined in the context of man's need to feel worthwhile. Is the morality of society declining or merely changing?

The moral fibre of the British people

Victorian Britain had its own methods for controlling idleness and the avoidance of work on some invented or exaggerated pretext. Not only was unemployment and starvation a very real threat to the working classes but capitalist theologians provided spiritual support for the material necessity to work long hours in miserable conditions for a subsistence wage. Puritan doctrine branded idleness a grave sin and work a virtue. Any avoidance of work was said to be evil and even sickness was not always a valid reason for absence from work. The rewards for hard work and thrift (poverty) were promised in the next world but not, of course, in this one. The hypocrisy of such a doctrine appeared to pass unnoticed by the idle rich for whom, for some unexplained reason, the doctrine was turned upside down. It was positively unseemly for a lady of social standing to turn her hand to work. Western Capitalism thus developed by providing no choice to the working class but to support it. The threat of hunger and hypocritical promises spurred men on to spend their stunted lives creating other men's profits.

It is hard to take seriously the suggestion that the moral fibre of such a society is in any way strong. To work because of fear of starvation of oneself and one's family, the primary motivation until the formation of the welfare state – can hardly be described as noble or strong. It illustrates more simply the animal instinct in us all for self-preservation.

What has happened to the moral fibre of the British people today? Dr Rhodes Boyson assumes that it has been weakened, but the evidence suggests a change rather than a weakening of morality. Young people today are less materialistic and more thoughtful than they have ever been. No longer does it matter what a man or woman owns; what matters is what he does or doesn't do. It is no longer automatically accepted that a man should fight for his country right or wrong. If careful consideration of the issue at stake reveals that a war has not been forced on the home country, then men may stand out against authority and refuse to fight. America produced one million conscientious objectors against the Vietnam war. In similar circumstances Europe might well produce at least as many. Is such a stand a sign of a weakened moral fibre?

One set of values for the rich and another for the poor

Similar developments have occurred in attitudes to work. Increasingly men and women are not prepared to spend the majority of their working hours making other men's profits unless the job provides some satisfaction for themselves. Perhaps the questioning of the protestant work ethic arouses stronger feelings amongst the upper classes than any other aspect of the so-called permissive society. But one only has to ask when any upper class individual has been prepared to under-utilize his capacities for a lifetime undertaking unfulfilling, dirty and dangerous work to know just how hypocritical such criticisms are. Less today than ever before will the working class (or the younger members of it) accept one set of values for the rich and another set for the poor. If the middle class expects to find satisfaction at work, then the working class do too.

Much more understandable are the resentments of the middle age group of the working class who had little or no option but to accept any job offered to them in the circumstances of the 1930s depression, the war and the post-war period of austerity. Training schemes and optional extra years at school were beyond the wildest dreams of the average working-class boy or girl. Satisfaction at work was the privilege of the few and not even expected by most. Today it is the majority who expect to find their work fulfilling – a change that should surely be welcomed, not condemned as a sign of the depravity of the nation.

Perhaps the group where it is least accepted that they share the desire for a fulfilling job is that of the young, unskilled, unmarried men to whom the four week rule is applied. These men are assumed by the authorities simply to be unwilling to work, despite the availability of jobs.

The findings of our study, however, provide abundant evidence that the traditional image of the under forty-five, unmarried supplementary benefit claimant is wildly misleading.

Declared intentions to work or not to work

Of the men we interviewed:

1. Only 2 per cent wilfully avoided work and would prefer to remain out of work indefinitely if possible.

2. Fully 98 per cent of the sample wished to work all or most of the time: of these 83 per cent wanted to avoid any break at all between jobs; a further 10 per cent wanted to find a satisfying job and then remain employed permanently; the remaining 5 per cent of the sample would prefer to remain employed most of the time but to have a bit of extra holiday from time to time.

The latter 5 per cent consisted of men, usually skilled or with some academic qualifications, who were looking for a job for which they are qualified. These men were prepared to take unskilled jobs, but preferred the monotony of work to be broken by short periods of unemployment until an appropriate job was found. In a period of relatively full employment most of these men would have been employed on a permanent basis, but in 1972, when our interviews took place, the only available work in many areas was repetitive and boring in the extreme (e.g. potato peeling and sweeping up). As an actor explained: 'I'm not mad about peeling potatoes'.

Hopes and plans

More than a third of the sample (38 per cent) were either skilled workers or had some academic qualifications or a career in the arts, and of the rest of the sample a fifth intended to undertake a training or acquire a skill in order to find a more fulfilling job or to achieve greater security at work. 'I'm taking a course in car body work and spraying. I want to have a skill and get a good job', said one young man who had already had enough of unskilled work at the age of twenty. Another avenue of escape from boredom and poverty appears to be emigration: a quarter of the remaining unskilled or semi-skilled men intended to go abroad to find a better job than they expected to find in this country. We are left then with less than one third of the sample of so-called 'workshy' individuals who had unskilled or semi-skilled jobs at the time of our interviews and who had no plans to go abroad or to train or acquire a skill.

Contrary to the suggestion that the provision of state benefits is causing a collapse of men's interest in work and an ever increasing readiness to sit back and accept state help, the motivating force of the men interviewed is to maintain their independence, to improve themselves, 'to get any job with good pay and good prospects', 'to get any hospital clerical job – I want to work helping people', 'to become a hairdresser', 'to get a job with good money so I can bring myself up a bit, gain more confidence to hold a good job', 'stay in work and get a couple of horses – I like horses and racing', 'work till I get enough money to start a firm of my own with a friend'. 'Run a firm for 2–3 years then probably go to New Zealand – they give grants towards starting a business there'. 'Get a decorating contract in Britain – work and save up for a cottage'. Only seven who were dissatisfied with present work prospects explained that they had no plans to improve the situation.

As already mentioned, two claimants were alone in taking an entirely negative view towards work:

(1) I don't want to work at all. I like meeting the mates and going down to the betting shop –

and (2) I won't work. Apart from that – I don't know what I'll do.

And the remaining five regarded plans as a rich man's privilege: 'If I had the money, I would go to the South Pacific. People have plans if they have money – all you can do on social security is to survive.' The feeling of hopelessness and resignation shared by all five was expressed clearly by one: 'With no qualifications I can only get labouring jobs. I only ever get offered about £12 per week. One day I'll have to settle down, but I don't know what I'll do. If only I could get a really satisfying job to satisfy my mind and soul.' Even if there is not the opportunity to find some fulfilment at work, the yearning for it is apparent.

Attempts to find work during a period of unemployment

At the time of our interviews the level of unemployment in Britain was at an unprecedentedly high level and more than half of the respondents interviewed were unemployed in the period March to September 1972 when officially recorded unemployment reached 4·5 per cent of all employees, a figure probably representing about $1\frac{1}{2}$ million persons, when unofficially unemployed persons are taken into account. A further quarter were unemployed in the latter half of 1971 when unemployment was already on the increase and only a small minority referred in their interviews to periods of unemployment in relatively easy employment situations. The worsening of the unemployment situation in 1972 is illustrated by the average number of jobs offered by the employment exchange in 1972 compared to the preceding period. In 1972 claimants were offered on average only 1·4 jobs during their period of unemployment whereas those who had been unemployed prior to 1972 were offered on average three jobs each by the employment exchange. Similarly if we consider the total number of jobs applied for during the period of unemployment, two-thirds of those who had applied for less than five jobs were unemployed in 1972, whereas these applicants who had applied for ten or more jobs tended to be those unemployed before the crisis 1972 year. Despite the fact that the employment exchanges in 1972 were unable to offer a single job to twenty-one of the claimants, all but three of these men had applied for a number of jobs of their own accord, and three applied for more than ten jobs during the period of unemployment.

Not only are the unemployed often accused of not trying to find work, but they are often said to be unwilling to travel. Once again it seems that the rest of society is too harsh – fully a third of our sample had applied for jobs involving a journey of more than three-quarters of an hour each way. Bearing in mind the cost of that amount of travelling to the majority who were unskilled or semi-skilled, the evidence suggests a remarkable willingness to travel.

The above facts bear out the very limited evidence already available concerning the attitude of unemployed men to work. For instance an independent observer inquiry suggests that the proportion of the working population (excluding the mentally or physically sick) who elect to remain at home when work is available is in the region of 0·03 per cent (*Observer*, 15.9.68). And, as already mentioned, the most thorough survey of the problem ever undertaken by the N.A.B. (in 1965) found that of 32 000 men and women interviewed who had been unemployed for two months or more and were drawing benefit, only 7 per cent were considered 'workshy'; and over three-fifths of this 7 per cent were physically or mentally handicapped.

Indeed, what has been remarkable in the past has been the willingness of millions of unskilled men and women to spend the bulk of their working hours doing some meaningless task in return for a pittance of a wage, with less security than was enjoyed by the rest of the community, less status, less power, less pension rights, worse health, and worse working conditions probably also compounded at home with inferior housing, inferior schooling for the children and so on. But in cases where this deal is just not accepted, three means have been developed for coping with the failure of employers to consider adequately the needs of their employees. These are short periods of employment and frequent changes of employment, absenteeism, and an opting out of the established fields of employment.

Adjusting to the system

Short periods of employment. Of our sample of ninety-eight men, 15 per cent expressed a desire for short periods of unemployment between jobs so long as they continued to be confined to unskilled work. As already mentioned, four-fifths of these men had specific plans for attaining more skilled and interesting work, and anticipated that they would wish to work continuously once they had found a fulfilling job, but it is worth noting that a less 'responsible' attitude to work was readily admitted by men, many of whom had some academic qualifications, who could not stand permanent unskilled work.

A further reaction of young people to unacceptable work situations is to change from one job to another at frequent intervals. Only nine of those interviewed had held only one job, whereas nearly one-fifth had held a series of jobs for periods averaging less than three months. The data may be summarized as follows:

Average time for which jobs have been held in the past

% of men	Average length of time
18	less than 3 months
21	3–5 months
15	6–8 months
20	9–12 months
17	longer
9	only one job held
100%	

Frequency of job changes increases not surprisingly as you move down the occupational scale, and can be expected to increase amongst unskilled workers as more young people leave school with inquiring minds and developed talents.

Absenteeism. On the Continent a situation of industrial unrest characterised by strikes, high rates of absenteeism and restrictive practices is generally called the English Sickness. Our own press has been eager to give publicity to an apparent explosion in absentee rates, and one might well be inclined to wonder whether the moral fibre of the British workers has in fact been weakened over recent years.

In fact an enquiry into the sickness absence figures of nine countries with full records since the early 1950s revealed that between 1955/6 and 1967 the English sickness absence figures had increased to 110 per cent of the base line, while in Sweden the rise had been to 140 per cent, in Italy to 138 per cent, in Holland to 135 per cent and West Germany to 128 per cent – all well above the increase in Britain. The US and Poland had experienced rises very similar to our own, and only Yugoslavia and Czechoslovakia have experienced scarely any rise at all.

The enquiry confirms the observations made by industrial medical officers in the past few years, that sickness absence is becoming much more frequent and that this is most obvious in episodes lasting from a day or two up to a fortnight.

'The Italian analysis is particularly interesting since it shows clearly that most of the rise in sickness absence since 1949 has taken place amongst industrial employees, and that the rise in the commercial sector has been smaller, while rates in agriculture have been changed little. I would suspect that the same thing has taken place here, although our national figures are not broken down in this way. The evidence suggests that rising rates of sickness absence are characteristic of the industrial societies in which we live' (**P. Taylor,** *The English Sickness in Industrial Society,* July 1970, p. 8–26) (from *Social Problems of Modern Britain,* eds. E. Butterworth and D. Weir, Fontana 1972).

The medical conditions causing absence have changed markedly over the past fifteen years, e.g. there has been a substantial fall in the days attributed to tuberculosis, dermatitis, peptic ulcers and kidney disease. On the other hand, sprains and strains of muscles and joints have been responsible for a three-fold increase. The slipped disc and diarrhoea follow close behind. Psychological disorders, diabetes, coronary heart disease and bronchitis also account for the increase. A substantial element of the increase in the last three conditions can be attributed to improvements in treatment and medical care which prevent early death, but often keep the patient alive in a constantly imperfect state of health. The point that has been made is that the main causes of the increase in sickness absence (sprains, slipped discs and diarrhoea) have few objective signs which can be detected. Backache is most difficult to confirm or disprove and only in the Forces is proof of diarrhoea required before a soldier is released from duty. How much sickness is either fabricated or exaggerated? It is impossible to say, but common sense can tell us that if a man is forced to work in an unsatisfying job for little or no net gain over and above the level of National Insurance benefits that he would receive when sick, a bit of backache will be grasped as an excuse for a rest more readily than if he had some motivation to work.

It cannot be argued that absenteeism is a result of the welfare state and the provision of benefits without adequate safeguards against abuse. The simple fact is that no sickness benefit is paid for the first three days of sickness unless an individual remains sick for more than twelve days, in which case benefit can be reclaimed for the initial three days. The worker who fails to show up at work on a Friday, or for three days during Whit week, will receive no payment for his lost hours of work. Absenteeism merely signifies the increasing value placed on leisure as against money and it exists as a problem in all the leading industrialized societies.

We read so much about absenteeism in the press, but little is said about the substantially smaller number of holidays to which the British worker is entitled when compared to his European counterpart. In Germany, for instance, twenty-four working days off is more or less the rule, and nearly half as many 'Freitage' in addition. Many Italians get as many as thirty public holidays, and the French have eighteen. The British worker works four weeks a year more than his American counterpart and nine weeks a year more than the Swedes (*Observer*, 13.4.69). Employers should not be surprised when workers take the law into their own hands and take *unpaid* holidays in the form of protest strikes or 'sick' leave.

Opting out. One growing group in society, the hippies, the drop-outs, opt for a life style which represents a marked material contrast to the values of Protestant Ethic man. The odium of society extends more strongly to these individuals than to almost any other group in society and it is relevant to ask why. Are we threatened by those who succeed in rejecting utterly the values which we ourselves question and yet which provide the foundation for a secure and comfortable life? Are we threatened too by these who ask questions the answers to which we would prefer not to think about: for what and for whom do we work? For what are we living? What is the point of working at a boring job for the sake of *owning* more material objects? Is it not preferable to be happy at work earning just enough money to eat and to live simply?

Six of our respondents had found their own answers to these questions and intended to remain outside the official employment fields as far as possible and to try and make a living doing what they really wanted to do – singing, painting, leather work and, if necessary, occasional part-time jobs to bring in some extra cash.

A typical example of the group was Don – a tall, good-looking fellow with long curly hair who, with his musical and artistic talents, might expect to lead a rewarding existence. Instead, on leaving school with only 'four' O level passes, he was faced by the usual choice of clerical office work or factory work. By the age of twenty-four he had been through about ten jobs ranging from grill chef to swimming baths attendant, from foreman's clerk to plastics operator and finally to sweeping up for an upholstery manufacturer. The worst it seems was the plastics job where he suffered from the effects of fumes and plastic dust, but over the years it was the greyness and boredom which finally provoked an acute depression needing a year's psychiatric treatment, and resulting in a lengthy period of unemployment. Don claimed supplementary benefit which he received for four weeks. At the end of that period he applied for a continuation of benefit on the grounds that he could not live on his £4 unemployment benefit. He failed to explain his psychiatric condition to the officer since he felt 'it would do no good', and was denied any further benefits. Financial worries were thus added to his psychiatric problems and a few weeks later Don was arrested for selling cannabis. The provision of medical reports led to his release from prison, but 'no constructive help was offered' on how to survive on £4 a week.
At the time of our interview Don had recovered sufficiently to take a job and was prepared to take any jobs he could find in order to have the money to buy leather and other materials to begin work again on home-produced goods for sale in boutiques. The main problem, he said, was that he hadn't the confidence to take his goods round the boutiques but hoped in time to build up a little arts and crafts business, and also to play his guitar in clubs in the evening.

Don is no layabout but rather a man broken by his attempt to slot himself into the modern industrial machine. The drop-out is a recent phenomenon, so what, we might ask, would have become of Don fifty years ago? Two possibilities present themselves: either Don's creative talents may never have been developed, he may have found it easier to accept his 'lot' as a bored and pointless labourer. Alternatively he may have suffered throughout his life from a chronic depression resulting from a failure to fulfil his creative desires. Either way it would seem preferable that he has a chance to lead a satisfying existence which the affluence of modern society makes possible.

The morality of the 1970s was well summarized by Sir Edward Boyle M.P. when he said: 'I believe there is a higher incidence of courage and thoughtfulness among young people today on both sides of the Atlantic than ever before. Young people are fearless in trying to face themselves, and to discover a scale of values and of objectives with which they can feel truly identified. Moral considerations weigh strongly with them, but must be related to situations and choices which have relevance in terms of their own experience.'

The need for work

Why, if work has become so unfashionable, do only about 0·03 per cent of the population willingly remain unemployed when suitable jobs are available? The answer lies in the very deep psychological need of the average person to feel worthwhile. It is hard to feel worthwhile if one is sponging off a relative, friend or the State. Secondly the equally powerful need to have a sense of belonging; to be a part of a structure; to have a reason to get out of bed in the morning! If a man has no will to work in either an official or unofficial capacity, then he will almost certainly either turn to the criminal world with its own code of values and its own structure or he will collapse in a heap of depression. The concept of a lazy healthy layabout enjoying his leisure at the expense of the State is contrary to the very nature of man. Individuals may avoid work in the established sense and remain at home manufacturing bombs for the IRA, painting plaques of an Indian Guru, or contributing to any other cause they consider worthwhile, but such individuals are not layabouts – their system of values merely diverges from the norm. We have yet to discover a genuine layabout though two of our sample, members of the criminal fraternity, would give an impression of enjoying a leisurely though risky existence. Neither would, however, choose to be in the position of living off the State – they wanted to live on the proceeds of their own activities.

For the vast majority of the population (and for 98 per cent of our sample) employment for most if not all the time is a pre-condition of mental and physical health. The following graph illustrates the catastrophe which prolonged unemployment represents to many claimants. It cannot be argued that mental ill-health and sleeplessness are a direct result of the financial strains of loss of benefit because the symptoms were equally apparent amongst claimants who had not been deprived of benefit as they were amongst the less fortunate individuals. Only fourteen of the sample who were un-

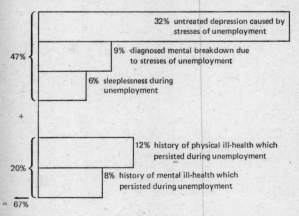

Incidence of Ill Health or Symptoms of Emotional Anxiety during unemployment

employed for more than six weeks managed to escape any mental or physical symptoms, a further four were officially unemployed and healthy but were outside the normally accepted definition of unemployed. Two were attending courses, one in mechanical engineering and the other in car body-work, a third was on holiday for eight weeks after his finals exams when he attained a degree in biology and the fourth was touring the Continent as a member of a pop group though receiving no wages (all the proceeds of the group were needed to cover the expenses of the tour and for investment in equipment).

Fully 81 per cent of those unemployed for more than six weeks complained of depression, sleeplessness, nervous breakdown or physical illness during their period out of work. This finding supports earlier evidence in a study of R. N. Antebi (*The British Journal of Psychiatry* (1970), **117**, 205–206, State Benefits as a Cause of Unwillingness to Work) which showed that all but one of his sample developed depression, sleeplessness, free-floating anxiety, headaches, shortness of breath or a number of other symptoms as well as various somatic complaints during their periods of unemployment. Both studies suggest a close relationship between unemployment and mental, emotional and physical complaints. The inescapable conclusion from these results is that voluntary unemployment is unlikely ever to become a major problem.

It may be true that with the present system of means-tested benefits and allowances unskilled men with several children have little or no financial incentive to work. However it is not money, but the desire to work, to be self-reliant and occupied, that limits the number of those seeking to evade the controls of voluntary unemployment to about 0·03 per cent of the employed population. Further evidence supporting this view is the attitudes of the men interviewed towards their period of unemployment. Nearly two-thirds of the sample (62 per cent) were more concerned about boredom during the period than they were about the limited amount of money at their disposal. If unskilled men, like the rest of the population, dislike unemployment, they are much more likely than any other group to dislike their work as well. The following graph illustrates the attitudes to work of different groups. Nearly half the skilled men were very satisfied with their previous jobs, whereas only 13 per cent of the unskilled men were as satisfied with theirs. On the other hand a third of the unskilled men were very dissatisfied with their previous job, compared with 20 per cent of skilled men. When all the disadvantages of low pay, low status, dirty and often dangerous

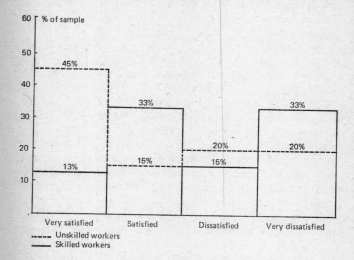

conditions and a minimum of fringe benefits are concentrated on unskilled work, dissatisfaction must be expected and the remarkable fact perhaps is that *so few* opt for anti-social methods (e.g. thieving) of escaping from the rut.

Money – the dominant incentive to work?

It is often supposed by the critics of modern morality that most people dislike work and do not work willingly so that in the absence of any real threat of unemployment (at least until 1971–2) the only powerful incentive to work is money.

Several careful studies however dispute this view. A study of 100 department store employees and 150 miscellaneous workers showed that good pay came sixth and seventh respectively on a list of twelve items. Opportunity for advancement came first and steady work second in both groups. (Chart 'Measuring the Factors that Make a Job Interesting', *Personnel Journal*, 1932, 11.)

Employees in a trading organization placed good pay twenty-first on a list of twenty-eight items. (J. D. Hauser, *What People Want from Business*.)

17 000 employees of Joseph Lucas Ltd. placed security first and high earnings fourth of seven items. (J. A. C. Brown, *The Social Psychology of Industry*, Penguin.)

The relative unimportance of money as a factor in assessing a job is somewhat less apparent from our own study – not surprisingly amongst generally low-paid workers. Nevertheless the nature of the work was more than twice as important as money in determining whether or not a man was satisfied or dissatisfied with the job he held prior to his period of employment.

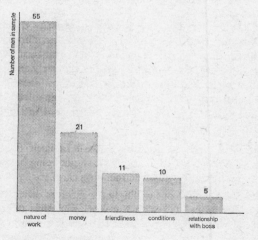

Factors influencing attitudes to a job

Of the eighty-five men who had been employed and who specified the reasons for their attitude to their previous job fifty-five (or 65 per cent) explained that their dissatisfaction was due to the boring nature of the work, the lack of any responsibility, the lack of variety, etc., or that their satisfaction was due to the opposite qualities of the work itself: the variety of tasks; the fulfilling or rewarding nature of the work, the freedom to 'make my own decisions', and so on.

Money was a factor determining the attitude of less than a quarter of the men, but the evidence of this study supports the view held by industrial psychologists that if wages are poor or unfair (e.g. if skilled rates are not paid for skilled work), then this can be an important cause of discontent. For instance, a skilled metal welder explained that his take-home pay of £17 per week in 1972 was not a skilled wage. In 1971 an unskilled labourer in London claimed that his take-home pay was £11 per week and, even more cause for complaint, a skilled carpet fitter was taking home £10 per week in the same year. These men and others were bitter that advantage was being taken of the poor employment prospects of workers in order to hold down wages.

But despite the hard employment situation of the years in question the conditions of work and the friendliness of the atmosphere at work were together as important a criterion of satisfaction as was the money factor. Particularly amongst the unskilled men, outdoor work and the friendliness of their mates ranked high as did the variety of tasks involved in a job.

These various motives may be summarized in three types of motive for working:

1. The work may be done as an end in itself (e.g. a car mechanic who didn't mind about the wages being below those for some other jobs – he loved mending cars).

2. It may be carried out willingly for motives other than (1), but directly associated with the work situation (e.g. a soft drinks salesman who explained that the main reason why he had enjoyed his job was the fact that he was top salesman).

3. It may be carried out for genuinely extrinsic motives (e.g. to obtain money used for a hobby, for the family or for a chance to escape from the particular job and setting up in business on one's own. Don the artistic leather worker for instance was motivated to take an unskilled job for this last reason).

Men are motivated only by money to the extent that employers have failed completely to satisfy the first two types of motive, because only then does the third type of motive become important. But increasingly employers are aware that a repetitive job can be satisfying if three conditions are fulfilled:

1. That the value and significance of the job to the firm and to the community are understood, and

2. if the conditions of work are favourable, i.e. that noise is limited and proximity of workers is ensured so that conversation and other social distractions can take place, and

3. that a variety of tasks are undertaken by each worker.

Only the really frustrated worker will seek money above all else: the worker asked to perform a meaningless repetitive task, and separated by noise or distance from his fellow workers. Or alternatively a worker performing a job which is sufficiently exacting to demand constant attention without being demanding enough to be interesting. It is in these circumstances that money is all that a man gets from his work and he will then do anything in his power to get all the money he can. The demand for more money may stem from a feeling of dissatisfaction combined with the notion that nothing can be done about it and the conclusion that 'if I've got to be bored all my working life, I'll get out of it what I can and make the best of my hours off'. A resort to motive three if all else fails.

However industrial discontent is expressed, the fact remains that money is not the main motivation to work. Men work in order to live, and to achieve a sense of satisfaction, to feel useful, wanted and to attain a social status. And as Lord Beveridge said, 'the greatest evil of unemployment is that it makes men seem useless, not wanted, without a country' rather than any financial loss involved.

5 The Effects of Loosely Worded Rules

I lived off my wits, my girl friends and stealing things.

It is suggested by the Supplementary Benefits Handbook that for the individual claimant the discretionary powers of the Supplementary Benefits Commission 'may be more valuable than a precisely prescribed right because they give the scheme a flexibility of response to varying situations of human need'. In an ideal situation there is every reason to believe that flexibility is preferable to rigidity for any service seeking to meet the almost infinite variety of individual human needs.

However, in the context of a value-ridden society with strong feelings of antipathy towards the recipients of state benefits, with the staff under extreme pressure due to staff shortages and with poor conditions of work and an ever-increasing burden of work, it is important to consider the effects on the individual claimant of loosely worded rules and discretionary powers.

The handling of skilled men

The vagueness of the instructions to Supplementary Benefit Officials is perhaps at its worst when determining who will be treated as a skilled man. This is of some importance to the people concerned when skilled men are allowed a period up to three months in which to find a suitable job before their benefit is withdrawn, whereas unskilled men are allowed only four weeks.

If the following three extracts from the Supplementary Benefits Handbook are considered it is perfectly clear that an official may interpret the rule in three very different ways: (1) allowing everyone except the completely unskilled a full three months if necessary before withdrawing benefit; (2) withdrawing benefit after four weeks from all except those with unusual skills and many years of experience; or (3) allowing unemployment of anything between four and twelve weeks to people depending on their age and degree of skill before withdrawing benefit.

Extracts from the Supplementary Benefits Handbook

For sympathetic officials

'Para 170. In areas where unskilled work is available, supplementary benefit is granted for four weeks only to fit men who are single, *unskilled* and under age 45. The unskilled claimant should be able to find work within four weeks, will be expected to do so, and the Commission *might* refuse further benefit after that period.
Para 172. Only if a skilled man continues to draw supplementary benefit for at least three months will his entitlement be challenged.'

For less sympathetic officials

'Para 168. The more skill and experience a man has in his chosen occupation, the longer he should be allowed to seek such work before being urged to consider alternatives.'

For unsympathetic officials

'Para 170. At this early stage of a claim (i.e. at the outset) labouring work or portering is not of course regarded as suitable for a man who has a *special* skill such as a trained craftsman'. (Can this statement be interpreted to mean that potato-peeling *is* 'suitable' for a young bricklayer or engineer?)

If an officer wishes to give a skilled man a full three months (if necessary) to find a job appropriate to his training then he clearly has the authority to do so. Providing the four week rule is not imposed at the outset then a skilled man will receive a more careful consideration of his case than is allowed for an unskilled man. Whereas an unskilled man will cease to receive benefit after four weeks *unless he* returns to the office to renew his claim, in the case of the skilled man the initiative has to be taken by the officers before benefit can be withdrawn (if the rule is correctly applied). The Handbook explains the procedure for skilled men in some detail: 'A claimant who has been drawing a supplementary allowance for about three months is asked to come to the local office for interview'. 'This interview provides an opportunity for a full discussion with the claimant of his efforts to find work, of the additional steps he might take to find himself a job, of any difficulties which may be preventing him from doing so and of any ways in which he could be helped. If it is clear that he is not really trying to get a job, he is warned that he has a liability to maintain himself (and his dependants, if any) and that his allowance cannot be continued indefinitely while he looks for the precise job he would like as opposed to the kind of job which may be available for him'. It is only at this interview that a skilled man may be told that his allowance will be continued for four weeks only and might not be renewed.

If interpreted generously, therefore, the four week rule provides ample time for skilled men to find a suitable job before benefit is withdrawn.

What happens in practice?

Fully one-fifth of our sample were skilled men to whom the four-week rule had been applied at the outset of their claim. If this were nationally representative, it would suggest that of the quarter of a million men to whom the rule has been applied throughout the country since 1968, probably about 50 000 have been skilled. This fairly indiscriminate application of the rule to skilled men at the outset of their claim or within 2–3 weeks of the outset is surely contrary to the spirit of the Handbook and to the intentions of the Minister who introduced the rule in 1968. But so large are the numbers that it must leave open the question as to whether the rule was intended in practice to apply to skilled men, at least in certain wide-ranging categories.

Moreover, it appears that if an error is made at the initial interview, this is unlikely to be rectified if a skilled man returns to the office after four weeks to appeal for an extension of benefit. Two-thirds of the skilled men who re-applied for benefit were refused any further help on the grounds that they were entitled to benefit for only four weeks and that they would have to find a job. In the few successful cases, it appeared to be the inability of the claimants to find any work despite a willingness to try that persuaded the officers concerned to extend the time for which benefit was granted. None of the skilled men had turned down 'suitable' skilled jobs, in fact all those who reclaimed benefit had applied for a number of jobs varying in number from two to about one hundred. But apart from the minority whose re-application for benefit was successful, such efforts to find work were ignored in the case of two-thirds of this group.

Treatment of skilled claimants – an example

The normal treatment of the skilled men in our sample may be illustrated by the case of an electrician who began his career as an apprentice and finished his training at college. Immediately after leaving college he claimed benefit while he looked for a suitable job. He was granted a supplementary allowance of £6 per week for three weeks, but it was emphasized at the *initial interview* that he would have to find work within that period. No mention was made of the possibility of reclaiming if he was unable to find suitable work within three weeks, and no suggestion was made that he should receive benefit for three months if skilled work was not available. Due to the wholly false impression given to the electrician as to his right to benefit, he took a less skilled job than he had prior to his college training, in a factory operated entirely on immigrant labour with appalling conditions. His simple explanation for taking the job was: 'I was forced into it, wasn't I?'

An exception to the rule?

The skilled claimant who received the most generous treatment and that approaching most closely to the Handbook stipulations was a mechanic living with his widowed mother. This claimant drew supplementary benefit for fully ten weeks before it was withdrawn, although he was told at the initial interview that he would receive benefit for four weeks only. However, in the following respects even this claimant was deprived of the full benefit to which he was entitled:

1. His weekly income was supplemented to the extent of 39p to bring it up to £3·71p a week. His entitlement was £5·80p a week.

(a) The gross sum was reduced because he was not a householder, but no account was taken of the fact that he was living with his widowed mother who was not in a position to keep her son.

(b) His allowance was further reduced because he 'left his employment voluntarily'. However, supplementary benefit may only be reduced for a period of six weeks on these grounds, and not for a full ten week period.

2. The claimant was not granted benefit for the full three months suggested in the Handbook.

3. He was not called for interview prior to the withdrawal of benefit.

When the claimant was unable to pay his mother the £5 he normally gave her for his keep, he made plans to leave home and went to live with his sister who was expecting her third child at the time. He then returned to the social security office to explain that he had a rent to pay and his benefit was restored at a higher level than he had received earlier, though still below the statutory level. Now in this example it must surely be recognized that his widowed mother needed money towards her son's keep at least as much as the claimant's sister needed that money. How are such inconsistent decisions made? The explanation would appear to lie in the discretionary powers of Supplementary Benefit Officials as to what circumstances justify the reduction of benefit; and also the exercise of discretion in determining what is meant by the term 'skilled man'.

If the examples of the electrician and mechanic were isolated, they might be of little consequence, but when, as already mentioned, one-fifth of the men to whom the four week rule applied in a similar fashion were skilled, the implications of the policy are of some significance. Half the skilled men who had found a job at the time of our interviews were in less skilled jobs than they had prior to their period of unemployment. If the aim of the Commission is to force skilled men into any job within four weeks of their becoming unemployed, then this should be made clear to the public. If on the other hand additional time is to be granted for skilled men to find appropriate work, then this should be made clear to the staff in order to avoid the sizeable proportion of 'errors' suggested by this study.

A better deal for the professional group

Professionally qualified men fared rather better at the hands of the Supplementary Benefits Commission. Three of the eleven, although threatened with the four week rule, nevertheless had their benefit continued without interruption after the end of the four week deadline. Six others reclaimed successfully: the dominant factor in their fortunes with the Supplementary Benefits Commission seemed to be their confidence and determination to ensure that the rules were adhered to. The men with less in the way of certificates and degrees to wave at the officials often lacked the confidence necessary to challenge their decisions and thus to obtain what was rightfully theirs.

The handling of the disabled

According to the Handbook the four week rule applies only to those who are free from any serious physical disability and who have shown no signs of mental disorder or instability. This apparently straightforward instruction allows very considerable discretion to the counter clerks who have to decide in each case whether or not a claimant has a *serious* physical disability or *shows* signs of mental disorder or instability. As one claimant aptly said: 'they don't count a damaged hamstring tendon as a disability – if you only have one leg, they'd count that', the suggestion being that only the most glaring disabilities are accepted as presenting a problem.

It is argued by the Supplementary Benefits Commission that every claimant is asked whether he is disabled. However a drug addict or a mental depressive does not think of himself

as being a disabled person. Secondly, every claimant is asked,
according to the official form, whether he has ever had a
considerable gap in employment due to illness or injury.
Since the aim of the interview is to establish whether or not
the claimant is genuinely in need (or 'a member of the deserv-
ing poor' as the cynical might put it), there is a natural
tendency on the part of the claimant to minimize the length of
periods of unemployment. What is meant by a *considerable*
gap in employment? A claimant who had been for several drug
cures, the most recent hospital stay having lasted a full year,
mentioned to the clerk that he had been in hospital, but was
not asked to give further details, so did not do so, and the
four-week rule *was* applied to him. Is a twelve month period
of unemployment due to illness not regarded as considerable?

Benefit withdrawn regardless of ill-health

Fully twenty-eight in our sample of ninety-eight men subject
to the four-week rule suffered from a mental or physical disability or illness which the writer would consider hindered
their ability to obtain and hold a job. Nine of these men
admitted their ailments to the social security officer at the
initial interview, but with no effect (all were threatened with
the withdrawal of their benefit after four weeks). The consequences can best be illustrated with an example.

A young ex-soldier, who had been injured while serving in Cyprus
and thus unable to do heavy work, was suffering from chest trouble
while unemployed (he explained that he had been coughing blood
and felt perpetually very cold and tired at the time). He described
his medical problems to the Social Security Officer who merely
remarked: 'I can't help that – it is nothing to do with me'. After
receiving benefit of £7 for three weeks, he was warned that his
benefit would be terminated. In fact because 'there was no work
about', his benefit was continued but reduced to £3 per week for a
further three weeks before being finally stopped. No concession
was made to enable him to recover his health before being plunged
into a state of destitution. Furthermore the four week rule was
applied to this young man in Wolverhampton between January and
March 1972 despite the fact that the national unemployment rate

at that time reached the unprecedented level of 6·9 per cent.
(*Department of Employment Gazette*, March 1972, page 289.)
In every area except London and the South East the unemployment
rate exceeded the level considered prohibitive as far as the four-week
rule was concerned in earlier years.

The ex-soldier had been paying a £6 rent for a furnished room. He
had no unemployment benefit and no savings behind him. He had
left his job after an argument with the boss to avoid being sacked,
but until the argument occurred had thoroughly enjoyed his work.
He paid heavily for that argument – he was unable to find another
job for six months during which he 'lived off his wits, his girl
friends and stealing things'. While he continued to receive
supplementary benefit, he managed to pay his rent by playing
classical music in cafés and selling his belongings, but once the
money stopped altogether, he started breaking into phone boxes
and stealing – 'there was nothing more I could do – girls go on the
streets or commit suicide, but a man just steals to keep alive'. This
led him into trouble with the police and a period of probation,
until finally he found a job, albeit a less skilled and lower paid one
than any held previously. 'Nevertheless I was chuffed to get it', he
said. 'When you're desperate, you don't bother what the job is.'
Perhaps this is the attitude aimed at by the Supplementary
Benefits Commission.

The remaining eight men who admitted their medical
problems to the social security officer were little or no more
successful than the ex-soldier. Only three ignored the threat
and reapplied for a continuation of benefit; two succeeded in
providing sufficient evidence that they had been seeking work
and were granted a continuation of benefit. The fact that in
one case the Employment Exchange had been unable to send
the claimant for a single job was apparently insufficient proof
of the difficult job situation at the time; secondly, the nervous
debility of one claimant and the leg injury of the other were
apparently not taken into consideration at all. The sole
criterion upon which the social security decision was made was
proof of efforts to find work. The third claimant who returned to the officer after four weeks to reapply for benefit
was suffering from a nervous breakdown for which he was
receiving treatment, but also had chronic bronchitis and
asthma which contributed to a poor work record. Despite all

this his re-application was refused. The remaining six men didn't return: four were still out of work after four weeks, but a fifth, despite his bronchial condition, took a factory job for one day, felt ill as a result of the heat in the factory and left. He was then able to receive supplementary benefit for a further four weeks by which time he found a more suitable job.

The impression given in every case is that the four week rule is applied regardless of the health of the individual or the availability of suitable jobs.

The importance of the relationship between officer and claimant

Seventeen of the claimants did not convey to the social security officials that they were suffering from mental or physical illnesses or injuries. Of these, ten were suffering from acute depression, anxiety states, drug addiction, nervous breakdowns or other mental illnesses sufficiently serious to require medical treatment. Here the relationship between officer and claimant is of some considerable importance and it is perfectly obvious that the conditions and particularly the lack of privacy and pressure of work in social security offices, and the attitude of the public towards mental illness which inevitably affects social security clerks as much as everyone else, prevent a frank discussion of a claimant's problems from taking place.

When asked why they had not explained their medical condition to the social security officer, the men concerned tended to give replies typified by the following two; either 'he would have just laughed at me – he wouldn't be able to understand I was serious', or alternatively: 'they don't listen. They see too many people; they are only interested in the paper work'. These comments together sum up one of the most serious consequences of discretion within the social security system. *Discretion puts a very heavy responsibility on those with the power to use it. Prejudices of the officers and likes or dislikes of individual claimants can affect the treatment given to these claimants determining in fact whether or not his livelihood is withdrawn.* As one young man put it: 'If your face fits, you're all right'. Or another who made an effort to look smart when he went up to the social security office: 'if you go up there in rags, they'll help you – it doesn't pay to make an effort to look decent.'

In this context can we be satisfied that the four week rule applies only to those 'who have shown no signs of mental disorder or instability'? If claimants conceal such disorders and if officers haven't the time or inclination to find out the medical history of claimants, it seems clear that this punitive rule will continue to be applied as readily to the sick as to the healthy.

The Department of Health and Social Security recognised this problem in a statement in February 1970 which said: 'It can well happen that when a man is labelled "workshy", it turns out that he has some physical handicap or that he is suffering from a mental illness or form of personality disorder which may explain his inability to find a job and settle down to it'. The statement goes on to admit that 'it may take patient investigation in some depth to get at the root of the trouble'.

Clearly the brief meeting at which it is decided whether or not to apply the four week rule does not allow 'patient investigation at some depth' into the claimant's problems. In answer to this allegation in the past the Supplementary Benefits Commission has asserted that not every claimant is a newcomer to a local office. Indeed this is true, but it is clear from this study that second and subsequent visits to the office hardly increase the mutual understanding between clerk and claimant. The majority of claimants with chronic mental or physical problems had experienced more than one period of unemployment, and the impression given is that a harsher attitude is taken to people who have received help on previous occasions.

For instance six of the mentally or physically sick claimants had been unemployed on five or more previous occasions. All these men reapplied for supplementary benefit when the four week period ended, and all were refused any further help. Furthermore, taking the sample as a whole, the 'regulars' were substantially *less* likely to have their benefit extended beyond the four week period than were those unemployed for the first time. We cannot conclude therefore that familiarity with sick claimants is of any benefit to them.

Whatever the obscure logic of the Supplementary Benefits Commission, there can be no doubt that the Minister when introducing the rule had no intention of applying it to men suffering from the ailments and disabilities listed in the following table:

Disabilities of claimants to whom the four week rule had been applied

Claimants who reclaimed unsuccessfully after 4 weeks	Claimants who did not reclaim though unemployed at end of four week period	Claimants who reclaimed successfully after four weeks	Claimants who found a job within four weeks	Claimants threatened with four week rule but whose benefit continued uninterrupted
Nervous breakdown (1)	Chronic bronchitis (1)	Leg injury (2)	Chronic bronchitis (1)	Mental illness (2)
Bone injury (1)	Ulcer (1)	Chest complaint (1)	Spinal injury (1)	Knee injury (1)
Chronic bronchitis (2)	Asthma (1)		Asthma (1)	
Weak heart following rheumatic fever (1)	Venereal disease (1)	Nervous disability (1)		
	Leg injury (1)			
	Agoraphobia (1)	Anxiety state (1)		
Drug addiction (1)	Chronic depression (1)	Mental illness (undefined) (2)		
	Ex-drug addicts still suffering physical effects of drugs (2)			

Since four-fifths of the sample were contacted outside Employment Exchanges, it is possible that the chronically sick and regularly unemployed are over-represented in this study. On the other hand, the men worst affected by the termination of benefit may not be included in our study: men who resorted to crime and were serving prison sentences at the time of our interviews and others whose mental disabilities were exacerbated by the financial strains, rejection by family and in some cases destitution which can result from the withdrawal of benefit, and who were languishing in mental hospitals unable to explain their plight. Taking these two factors into account, we can perhaps assume that a similar proportion of all four week rule victims are medically unfit as applied to our own sample. If this is the case some 55 000 men have probably been deprived of benefit when suffering from ailments inhibiting a return to work.

The question of the availability of local work

According to the Supplementary Benefits Handbook, the four week rule applies 'where in the view of the Department of Employment and Productivity there are good employment prospects for men seeking unskilled work'.

In 1968 the four week rule was introduced in all areas with the exception of Scotland, Wales and Northern England which, it was considered, did not have good employment prospects for unskilled workers. The employment levels in these areas were 3·7 per cent, 3·6 per cent and 4·6 per cent respectively in 1968. Since that time, as unemployment has fluctuated upwards in the country as a whole and to a varying extent in different areas, individual areas have temporarily ceased to operate the rule. Whether or not the rule operates at a particular office within an area or throughout an entire area is decided by the Supplementary Benefits Commission in consultation with the Department of Employment and Productivity. The officers concerned *use their discretion* as to whether or not local job opportunities are sufficient to warrant the exercise of the rule.

Under such arrangements, if the four week rule is applied

when no jobs are available in the area concerned, the claimant has no means of knowing whether a clerical error has been made. At least six of our sample, for instance, claimed to have been subjected to the four week rule during the last six months of 1972, when the rule was suspended in the six areas concerned. (The rule was suspended throughout the country during March 1972 and was only gradually reintroduced in succeeding months as employment opportunities increased.)

None of the six claimants (quite apart from several others who claimed no suitable work was available locally, but where this could not be checked for certain) questioned the legality of the application of the rule, though in several cases the consequences were far from those intended by the Supplementary Benefits Commission.

A Birmingham claimant lost his previous job due to a prison sentence. When he emerged from prison, he tried to avoid claiming any State help – 'I wouldn't have been seen dead in the Labour Exchange or Social Security Office at the time', he said. However after three weeks without money he went to the Labour Exchange who told him to complete a B.1 form and sent him to the Social Security Office. There he was granted £4·70 for four weeks; but was not told that he could apply for an extension if he remained unemployed after that date. With a national unemployment rate of 4·3 per cent, it is not altogether surprising that not only was this claimant still out of work after four weeks, but that his father, too, was out of work having been made redundant. He explained: 'I've been inside and was back to square one'. 'My girl friend is two months pregnant so I tried to get a job nearby, but there is nothing. At nights when I was walking home from her place I started doing a few break-ins and still do when I can.'

It seems that ex-prisoners are given a particularly cool reception at some Social Security Offices, but if an unconstructive attitude is taken in these circumstances, what chance is there of a man making a fresh start? 'I had been inside – fair enough – I was punished for what I had done, but while I was inside I worked hard, doing a full week's work. By law that should be my only punishment, but what happens? I am punished when I come out by not getting any unemployment benefit and by having my supplementary benefit cut'. To make matters worse, employers are naturally unenthusiastic about taking on ex-prisoners. The vicious circle seems inevitable.

However determined a man may be to 'go straight' after a prison sentence, he seems to have little choice but to resort to crime. Our Birmingham claimant stressed 'I *do* want to get a job – I've got to do something especially now that my girl friend is going to have a baby, but there is just nothing to be had round here'. 'I have been been very tempted to take drugs – at least I would feel on top of the world for even a few hours.'

After a break without benefit this claimant returned to the social security office and completed another B.1 form, and was granted benefit. Neither he nor the official mentioned his earlier period of unemployment and one has the distinct impression that his benefit was renewed by a mistake – due to a failure to realize that the four week rule had already been applied to the claimant, just as his benefit had originally been terminated in error!

The remaining five cases of withdrawal of supplementary benefit in 1972, when the rule had been suspended in the areas concerned, had somewhat less serious consequences. One was receiving unemployment benefit (though less than he received for four weeks including supplementary benefit) and another reclaimed successfully on the grounds that he was on the professional register.

A skilled welder in Stoke-on-Trent, however, was forced to leave home to take a job with a wage £17 per week below the skilled welder's rate. He could find no welding job and no job at all in his locality. He normally lived with his widowed mother and five school age brothers and sisters and contributed £9 per week to the running costs of the home. He explained that he did not wish to leave his mother on her own with the five children, but equally he did not want his mother to have money worries. Due to a doubly harsh ruling by the local social security office, however, applying the four week rule to a *skilled* man in an area where the rule had been suspended, he was forced into a choice between these two alternatives.

The remaining two claimants disallowed during January to March 1972 were living with their parents to whom they shifted the burden. The situation was particularly unfortunate in one of these cases where the mother was a widow herself depending upon state help.

How the four week rule affects the unemployment pattern

If the discretionary withdrawal of benefit is to be justified, then the vast majority of those denied benefit should be at work within days of the application of the rule. In fact one fifth of the sample found work within the four week period – a 20 per cent success rate it appears superficially. However, five of these twenty claimants were skilled or professional men who felt compelled to take less skilled work due to the threat of withdrawal of benefit; probably only for 5 per cent of the sample did the four week rule successfully urge them back into appropriate jobs within the four week period. Others who found work within the four week period would have done so anyway.

What became of the 80 per cent of claimants who remained out of work for more than four weeks? Only a quarter of the entire sample were aware as a result of their interview at the social security office that they could reclaim after four weeks, though in desperation a number of others did return to the office at the end of the four week period to explain their position. Very nearly half the sample (48 per cent) remained out of work at the end of the four week period and either reclaimed unsuccessfully for a continuation of benefit or did not reclaim at all.

Of the men remaining unemployed beyond the four week period despite complete withdrawal of supplementary benefit, the average period of unemployment since withdrawal of benefit was seventeen weeks. It is important to note that twenty-one of the men were still unemployed at the time of our interviews, so seventeen weeks does not represent the average *total* length of unemployment without benefit, but only the average length of time up to the date of our interviews. Secondly, this figure excludes a professional thief who had been out of work for five years. In some cases men found work within two weeks of losing benefit, while others were without funds for anything up to seventy-six weeks. The following graph illustrates the distribution of the forty-nine men in length of unemployment (by number of weeks) *after* supplementary benefit was cut.

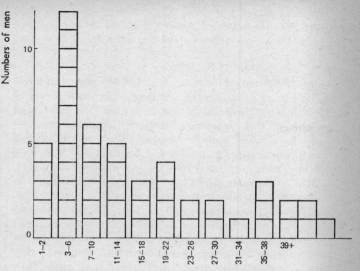

Number of weeks unemployed after Supplementary Benefit was cut

Social impact of the four week rule

The social effects of the withdrawal of supplementary benefit depended to some extent on the accommodation of the claimant – whether or not he was living with his parents; whether or not his parents were earning; and finally, if in rented accommodation, whether he was able to return home during the crisis. The following table summarizes this information:

Living with parents, with one or both parents earning   17
Living with parents – parents dependent on state benefits   3
Living in rented accommodation, and able to return home   4
Living in rented accommodation – not able to return home 24

    Of the entire forty-eight, only eleven reached a satisfactory agreement with their parents and remained out of trouble during the period without benefit. Three stayed with friends without apparent problems, but the remaining thirty-four either resorted to crime, suffered themselves or caused hardship to those around them. Yet only two of these men were not genuinely either sick or seeking work.

The incentive to resort to crime

Fully 24 per cent of the entire sample had resorted to crime in the past or did so for the first time during their period of unemployment reviewed in this study; and the substantial majority of these men were amongst those who remained unemployed when deprived of benefit under the four week rule (five succeeded in finding a job within the four week period or reclaimed successfully for an extension of benefits). *It is of considerable significance that of the twelve men who resorted to crime for the first time during their period of unemployment, eleven were amongst the forty-eight men remaining unemployed after benefit was cut.* Either due to the financial predicament caused by the loss of benefit or due to the bitterness caused by the withdrawal of benefit, the 'cut-off' group were very significantly more likely to resort to crime than those who retained supplementary benefit for the duration of their unemployment.

A typical example of the twelve men forced into crime has already been referred to earlier in this chapter:

The skilled welder of Stoke-on-Trent, living with his widowed mother and five younger brothers and sisters, had spent many years in hospital during his childhood and was not a fit person, though he did not suffer from any disability which would hinder his efforts to find a job. He was better able to explain his circumstances than some and made it clear that his criminal activities were prompted by his desperation to help his mother who, when his benefit was cut, spent the rent money on food for the five younger children.
'I started robbing when my benefit was cut because I could not afford to give my mother anything for my keep. Some weeks I couldn't pay her anything at all. I only used to eat one meal a day – that was when I came home in the evening. I had to help out as much as I could with the little money I got (from thieving) because all the children were still at school. I was still looking for a job hou gh – I went out each day to look for something'.

He finally found a less skilled job than he had been accustomed to with poor pay and work which he described as 'feeling like twenty-four hours when you were there for eight'.

The lack of food more than any other factor prompted men to steal. Some stole food directly, such as the young man who took boxes of tomatoes in the middle of the night from green-grocer shops after deliveries and who raided allotments for any food he could find, while others were prompted to steal saleable goods from offices or homes in order to eat. While those in rented accommodation were more likely to resort to crime than were those living with their parents, nevertheless four of the twenty-eight men living with their parents were sufficiently desperate for money to commit crimes for the first time in their lives. It is perhaps worth noting that these so-called criminals expressed more generous attitudes towards their parents and commanded the respect of the interviewers more than did a number of men who dealt with their predicament within the law. Should society punish a man who goes to the employment exchange religiously each day only to be told that no jobs are available in his line of work; a man who admits that he hates the idea of living off his parents and who resorts to breaking in for money to give his mother?

There is no reason to believe that the tendency to turn to crime is any greater amongst our sample of men than it would be amongst the four week rule victims in general. A possible bias in the other direction may have arisen if a number of those who resorted to crime feared an interview with us and therefore featured heavily amongst the 'refusals' for our study. *We can expect I think that approximately 12 per cent of four week rule victims, which would represent nearly 27 500 men since 1968, have committed crimes for the first time in their lives as a direct result of the withdrawal of benefit.* A further 25 000 men probably have a criminal history and are therefore more likely than others to turn to illegal methods of obtaining money if squeezed by the Supplementary Benefits Commission.

Claimants with a criminal history. It might be argued that men with a criminal history will turn to crime whether or not their benefit is withdrawn. The limited evidence of this study suggests that this may not be the case. Of the twelve men with a criminal history, seven returned to crime during their period of unemployment, and significantly six of them were still unemployed when their supplementary benefit was withdrawn. Four of the five who did not resort to crime, on the other hand, were more fortunate. One was back at work within the four week period as a result of the efforts of his probation officer on his behalf. Two successfully reapplied for benefit after the four week period; the fourth had only just been deprived of benefit at the time of our interview and planned to reapply. Only one man with a criminal history remained unemployed and without benefit and yet did not resort to crime. He moved in with a girl friend who was working and who met all his expenses and, it appears, the cost of drugs (he was an unregistered addict at the time).

It would seem, then, that the withdrawal o benefit was one of the crucial factors even amongst past criminals in determining whether or not they returned to illegal methods of obtaining money. Almost as important was the original level of supplementary benefit:

In the case of one young man living in rented accommodation, his benefit was insufficient – exceeding his rent by only £2·50 a week. He tried gambling, but lost more than he won, leaving himself with little or nothing with which to buy food. He did a bit of thieving before his benefit was cut, but things took a turn for the worse when he had no money at all for rent or food. 'It was terrible, I was really scratching around for money and sold everything I could until there was nothing left to sell. Then I met this older woman. She was older, quite a bit than me. She had quite a bit of money. We made a bargain – I had to make love to her, and she was not all that nice to look at in more ways than one! She wouldn't give me any actual money in case I cleared off, I suppose. So I used to nick it off her when she was asleep or drunk. It didn't keep up for very long because I didn't keep to my part of the bargain!'

A more direct link between the cutting of supplementary

benefit and a resort to criminal activities occurred in another case, that of a bright and very pleasant young man:

He felt extremely bitter when, despite trying every and any job available, 'even the dustbins – everything', he was deprived of benefit after six weeks. This young man accepted the notice of withdrawal of his allowance as a final 'no' and felt there was no point in reapplying. In fact, had he done so, he would almost certainly have had his benefit continued in view of the unemployment position at the time (October 1972) and in view of his obviously genuine efforts to find work. (One might perhaps wonder here, incidentally, about the apparent intention of the officer concerned to mislead the claimant into believing that there was no point in reapplying after six weeks. One might also question the legality of cutting total benefit to a level below the claimant's rent liability after only three weeks, leaving him with rent arrears and no money for food – this during a period of peak unemployment in 1972.) But whatever the technicalities, this young man temporarily resorted to crime as a direct result, he said afterwards, of the bitterness and desperation caused by the withdrawal of benefit even though such activities were so contrary to his normal way of life that he is unlikely to repeat them unless similarly pressed.

The cost to the tax payer of the four week rule. In addition to the inconvenience and loss to the persons against whom the crimes are committed and, more seriously, the social costs to the individuals propelled into criminal activities often with severe consequences for themselves and their families, what is the cost to the Exchequer of the four week rule in terms of probation officers' expenses, remand home and prison costs? The details provided by this study are inadequate to answer such a question, but it is worth noting that of ninety-eight claimants the following costs can be directly related to the operation of the four week rule:

1. A seven month stay in a mental hospital, followed by an unspecified period in custody while investigations were made.

2. An unspecified period of probation (in two cases).

3. Three weeks in Winson Green Prison (until medical reports justified his release).

4. Three months in a remand home, followed by probation.

The need for food. It has already been suggested that the need for food was one of the primary inducements to crime. One might have anticipated that each individual could turn to a parent, friend or relation for help and that hunger would not therefore be a serious problem. However, fully one-third of our entire sample explained that they were impelled to cut down on food, some drastically during their period of unemployment. All these men were living away from home and apparently unable to turn to their parents for help. Some were living with friends in a similar predicament. The idea that supplementary allowances cover the cost of rent, heating, food and other necessities is brought into question by the ᶠact that thirteen of the ninety-eight men in our sample complained of insufficient money for food while receiving benefit.

A glaring case of an inadequate allowance consisted in a weekly payment of £8·25p (including unemployment benefit) to a claimant with a rent of £8 per week to meet – the claimant's simple explanation of how to cope with the situation deserves a note: 'I just had to starve. I didn't eat for a couple of days and then had a meal and starved again, that's all. The electricity kept running out; food was so expensive and I had to pay 5p for a bath each time. I couldn't go out socially. I just put up with it'. This claimant remained unemployed for four weeks in 1972 and survived in his little furnished room in Bournemouth for four weeks with only 25p a week to spend.

The majority of men forced to cut down on food were those whose benefit was cut before they found work, and not surprisingly the seriousness of the situation varied considerably, depending upon the availability of friends to help out. Some managed by borrowing and cutting down generally on food; others were forced to limit themselves to one meal a day; while four of our entire sample (including the Bournemouth claimant) went without a meal for days at a time. Two of this last group resorted to stealing food, while six others avoided a starvation situation by thieving soon after their allowance was cut.

The following diagram summarizes the reasons, when given, for resorting to crime (it is important to note that we did not ask whether men had committed crimes, only how they made ends meet, and if they did admit to criminal activities, the questionnaire did not include questions as to why this was so).

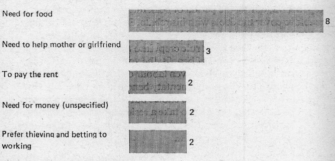

Need for food — 8

Need to help mother or girlfriend — 3

To pay the rent — 2

Need for money (unspecified) — 2

Prefer thieving and betting to working — 2

Justification for Thieving suggested by claimants

(2) *Effects of four week rule on parents and friends of claimants*

Of the forty-eight men who remained unemployed for at least a fortnight after being deprived of benefit, eleven relied entirely upon criminal activities to meet all their financial needs. Thirty-nine others however turned to parents or friends for help, and survived on an inadequate amount of unemployment benefit or shifted the burden in some way.

The parents of eight of the claimants were themselves sick, retired or unemployed and so unable to cope with the costs of an additional adult dependant. The results were in each case unfortunate and sometimes pathetic:

In one case a mother was drawing supplementary benefit when her son was deprived of benefit. He had purchased a suit on hire-purchase which he felt to be important when going for jobs. Rather than see her son take his suit to the shop, his mother took on the hire purchase repayments in addition to the general costs of feeding her son, thus reducing the standard of the two of them well below the poverty level.

Perhaps a more alarming case from the point of view of the use of discretion by Supplementary Benefit Officials is that of a skilled

builder-plasterer whose father had built up debts after contracting
a terminal illness. The young man left a job which he had held for
ten years at a wage of £55 a week in order to try and pay off the
family's debts with the help of tax rebates. He took this unwise
step in 1972, during the period of peak unemployment, and was
unable to cover the debts with his rebate. Some treasured family
possessions were sold and supplementary benefit kept the family
going – until the four week rule crept into this already unhappy
situation. When deprived of benefit, the young man claimed 'the
job situation was so bad that even labour officials could not offer
any hope of a job. The supplementaty benefit visitor couldn't help
either'. The ex-claimant had no choice but to leave the family and
leave his home town in order to take a residential dish-washing job
in an hotel. His main concern in doing so was the knowledge that
he might not see his father again.

How did the rule come to be operated on such a family at
such a time of peak unemployment and in such unfortunate
circumstances? Example after example of four week rule
cases raise the same question. Can discretion work under
existing arrangements?

Claimants living with their friends were more likely to have
medical problems and more likely to resort to crime than
those living with their parents. One might expect that men
with serious mental or physical problems such as drug
addiction, chronic depression, agoraphobia or venereal
disease would tend to remain at home with their families.
However, the majority of these men were living away from
home when their benefit was cut, and did not return home at
that time.

The question then arises as to whether the State should shift
the burden of the care of mentally sick people to individuals
in the community who receive no financial return. Why
should the parents of an agoraphobic claimant's girl friend
maintain and care for him? And why should he be forced
into such a position of total dependence? Why should flat-
sharers cover the rent of a colleague who contracts venereal
disease, loses his job and is deprived of benefit, when they are
also paying taxes to cover the cost of supplementary benefit
payments to others? If our system of social security means

anything, it must at least ensure a subsistence income to every individual unable for any reason to support himself. If the system does not provide that security, we are faced with a situation in which men have to 'beg' for their living; in which they are wholly dependent on the goodwill of relatives, friends or flat-mates who might turn them away at any time.

It appears from this study that parents are, if anything, less willing to accept the role of good samaritan to their adult sons than are friends. Rather more than half the four week rule victims who were living at home resorted to crime, felt the need to sell their belongings in order to pay their parents for their keep, or were impelled to leave home due to the ill-feelings aroused by their destitution. Ironically one claimant went so far as to sell his brother's clothes rather than ask for money direct from his parents. It seems that the Supplementary Benefits Commission cannot assume that a man living with his parents needs no financial help from the state.

The four week rule: what happens when there are children?

This survey concentrated on the effects of withdrawing benefit from single men under the age of forty-five. However, perhaps the most serious consequences result from the use of discretion where children are concerned. The four week rule may apply to married men (as well as to skilled workers and women) after a three month period of unemployment. But protection would appear to be given to children if we interpret correctly paragraph 172 of the Supplementary Benefits Handbook which says that the rule will apply 'unless there are dependants to whom this would cause hardship'. At the end of a three month period a married man should be called for interview, the official procedure being identical for skilled men and for married men. In the light of our findings that skilled men appear to receive exactly the same treatment as unskilled men, it might not be considered unreasonable to ask whether the same applies to married men with children. Are married men interviewed after three months or are they merely warned at the outset of their claim that benefit will be granted for four weeks?

No systematic evidence is yet available about the treatment of married men. We can only refer to individual examples such as the case of Mr Davison reported in the press recently (*Guardian*, 21.2.72).

'Mr Davison is married and has five children. After a long spell of unemployment, he found a job but lost it after three weeks. He renewed his claim for unemployment benefit and a supplementary allowance which was at first paid at the full rate of £15·25. After a few weeks however, it was reduced to £13 weekly. He was then called to the Department of Health and Security office and told that his supplementary allowance (£3·85) would be withdrawn after four weeks if he didn't get a job. He tried, failed, and the allowance was duly withdrawn. Within three weeks the family had received a distress warrant on a county court order for £4·50 and the baby was suffering from boils'.

It is hard to imagine any situation when the benefit of a married man with children can be withdrawn without causing hardship to the children, unless perhaps one believes that a man will sit at home and draw benefit when he could earn more money in a job. This point raises the very important question as to whether a man should be expected to take a job even if the wage offered is below subsistence level. The appalling dilemma very often faced by unskilled men with three or more children is that they cannot earn a subsistence wage except by doing many hours of overtime. During periods of high unemployment when overtime hours are sharply cut back, such men may be urged by their wives to remain at home in order to provide sufficient money (from the Social Security Office) to feed and clothe the children.

This leads to the question as to whether or not Social Security Officials try to force men into jobs with below subsistence wages by reducing or withdrawing supplementary benefit from the family. The Fisher Committee argued on this point that: 'We accept that a job should not be regarded as suitable if the net take home pay (plus family income supplement if applicable) is less than the weekly sum which the person will receive if he remains on supplementary benefit'. (*Report of the Committee on Abuse of Social Security Benefits*,

H.M.S.O. 1973, pp. 100 and 226.) Yet the Bradford Family Service Unit, for instance, has reported cases of men with six or seven children being urged into jobs with impossibly low wages (e.g. £13 a week in 1970) with an apparent disregard for the implications for the children in the families concerned.

The final chapter will be devoted to a discussion of a number of reforms which would overcome the dilemma that now faces large families with an unskilled breadwinner, the disabled and other low income groups as well as making possible a completely new role for social security offices.

Our discussion of the existing system would however be incomplete without a look at the problems faced by the people on the other side of the counter. What is it like to work for the Supplementary Benefits Commission for wages often very little above the benefits being paid out over the counter? Why is it that so many claimants appear to get a raw deal and why it is that suspicion so often exists between officer and claimant? Are the officers unreasonable people or are they just people in an unreasonable situation? Chapter 6 will examine this question.

6 Staff Problems and the Communication Gap

We have attempted in the earlier chapters to illustrate the effects upon claimants of a discretionary system of last-resort benefits. Public opinion is often critical of the 'over-generous' attitude of the State towards people assumed to be malingerers and layabouts. We have suggested that the public is over-reacting to a very small social problem in such a way that it forces the officials to over-react in their turn against the interests of the great majority of genuine claimants causing in many cases substantial hardship not only to the claimants themselves but also to their families, friends and to the victims of the illegal activities to which men turn in desperation.

The staff are caught in the middle of the cross-fire between the public and the claimant. They are instructed to combine two virtually incompatible aims:

1. To exercise their functions 'in such a manner as shall best promote the welfare of the persons affected by the exercise thereof' and

2. to control and detect abuse and to make economical use of available resources. Since the evidence suggests weaknesses in the *system* which should not be interpreted as weaknesses of the staff as individuals, it is important to analyse the problems facing the staff. Only then will the weaknesses in the system become distinct from any inevitable errors on the part of the staff operating under existing circumstances.

Staff shortage

From 1965 to 1971 the numbers of supplementary benefit staff increased by 75 per cent (from 12 468 to 21 224), while during the same period the number of claims increased by 150 per cent (from 2 847 000 to 6 428 000). These figures exaggerate the increase in work load due to the changing work routine, but taking all factors into account it is estimated by the Department of Health and Social Security that the work load has increased in real terms by 80 per cent during the period 1965–71. The current rate of increase in the numbers of staff inevitably means that inexperienced staff are recruited to fill new posts as well as to replace those who have left and who are promoted. There is therefore a dilution of experience resulting both from the loss of staff and from the expansion of demand made worse by the very high wastage particularly of clerical assistants.

Wastage: Overall permanent staff wastage and turnover on the social security side of the Department of Health and Social Security as a percentage of the staff in the four years 1967–1970.

	Year	Wastage	Promoted from the grade	Turnover
Executive	1967	5·3	2·3	7·6
Officer	1968	5·1	3·6	8·7
	1969	5·05	2·3	7·3
	1970	4·6	2·5	7·1
Clerical	1967	10·5	5·3	15·8
Officer	1968	9·2	3·2	12·4
	1969	9·8	3·7	13·5
	1970	12·0	2·7	14·7
Clerical	1967	15·6	10·8	**26·4**
Assistant	1968	15·2	9·7	24·9
	1969	20·4	9·7	30·1
	1970	21·4	10·5	31·9

Lack of experience

The proportion of inexperienced staff employed was revealed in a survey in 1968–9 of twenty-two local supplementary benefit officers. Fully 27 per cent of the executive officers interviewed had less than eighteen months' experience in the grade and 27·6 per cent of clerical officers had less than twelve months' experience. The Fisher Committee reported that in London the staff situation was particularly serious. It has not always proved possible to recruit sufficient qualified staff to keep London offices properly and fully manned, particularly in the clerical grades. There were 108 unfilled clerical officer posts in London local offices at the end of 1970 and a further 305 posts were covered by temporary promotion. To ease the excessive burden on the permanent staff at peak times, casual staff were employed to cover peak periods only. The number of casual man-weeks worked has increased almost three-fold since 1966, thus diluting still further the quality of work, and at the same time seriously affecting the morale of the permanent staff.

An excessive work-load

The 80 per cent increase in the real work-load of members of staff in a period of six years means that staff in local offices operate at a continuous level of overwork which 'makes it impossible for them to give claims the time and care which they require' (*Fisher Committee Report,* p. 179). The Department of Health and Social Security staff evidence to the Fisher Committee pointed out that 'we believe that claims for benefit, both in the home and in the local office are regularly taken in an atmosphere of pressure and hurry and often result in an unsatisfactory interview and an incomplete declaration of facts by the claimant. It is also true, of course, that this hurried type of interview sometimes results in the claimant's legitimate problems being glossed over and insufficient attention being paid to ensuring that all the requirements of the claimant are taken into account in arriving at a decision as to what benefit should be paid'.

It is hardly surprising in these circumstances that at least one of the witnesses to the Fisher Committee was unable to point to a single case where the four week rule had been operated in strict accordance with Supplementary Benefits Commission policy. Errors, misunderstandings, and failures to communicate vital details appear to be the rule rather than the exception and with a severe shortage of experienced staff this can be expected to continue. The situation does call into question the optimistic statement of Judith Hart when introducing the four week rule -- that 'there would be very real safeguards for the mass of genuine claimants', and that 'in the cases where the four week rule operated, there should be an experienced officer allocated whole or part-time to deal individually with the ones concerned'.

Why is the staff situation in Social Security Offices less satisfactory than in any other branch of the Civil Service when, as the Fisher Committee points out, the staff of local offices have a job which 'probably makes demands on officers of executive officer and clerical officer grades which are as great or greater than any in the Civil Service?' The answers probably lie in the pay, status and conditions of employees as well as in the almost impossible tasks faced by employees (a) of keeping pace with a constantly changing set of rules and regulations and (b) of combining the roles of policeman and welfare officer.

Staff training

The overwhelming emphasis of the Supplementary Benefits Commission upon economy and the control of abuse to the almost total exclusion of any concern for claimants as people, often with severe social as well as financial problems, becomes apparent in the training schemes outlined below.

Executive Officers when first employed or promoted are additional to their local office complement of staff for the first thirteen weeks of service. For the first ten weeks the trainee receives individual practical training in the office. Emphasis is placed on accurate assessment of entitlement and staff are taught by means of a series of self-teaching programmed learning texts. During the ten weeks experienced colleagues provide tutorials and introduce the Executive Officer to the basic technique of interviewing the public. For the last three weeks of initial training the course deals with a wide range of subjects, 'consolidating and expanding the basic knowledge acquired in the local office training. Detailed instruction is aimed at increasing technical expertise in such

List of Courses at Supplementary Benefit Training Centres

Course Management	Duration (Days)	Aim of Course
Higher Executive Officers and Senior Executive Officers transferred to supplementary benefit work.	5	To help officers who have supplementary benefit responsibilities to acquire the knowledge needed for the official management of the sections for which they are responsible. Sessions on fraud, liability of relatives and unemployment problems are included.
Executive Officers New entrants	20	To cover the duties of dealing with callers; home interviewing; assessment; and specialized subjects such as fraud; voluntary and long-term unemployment; overpayments; liability of relatives; appeals.
Newly-promoted	8	To define the officer's new responsibilities and to extend knowledge of caller and home interviewing; assessment and specialized subjects; fraud; voluntary and long-term unemployment; overpayments and liability of relatives; appeals.
Refresher	5	To establish the responsibilities and duties of the executive officer; to give advanced training in visiting and dealing with callers, and in assessment, to discuss specialist problems including liability of relatives, fraud, prevention of abuse, overpayments and voluntary and long-term unemployment; appeals
Liable relative specialist	4½	A course for specialist officers covering the technical and legal aspect of this duty; recovery from liable relatives; fictitious desertion and undisclosed cohabitation; interviewing; dealing with Courts.

Clerical Officers	15	To equip the clerical officer to carry out his duties in a local office; covering dealing with callers, assessment, overpayments, liability of relatives, voluntary and long-term unemployment so far as appropriate to clerical officers. The final five days of the course deals with home interviewing and may be taken as a separate course when proceeding to visiting duties. Throughout this course stress is laid on good interviewing techniques and verification, in the prevention of abuse.
Receptionist	1	To give instruction on the duties of a clerical officer acting as receptionist in an area office, including guidance in dealing with a variety of callers, e.g. itinerants, voluntary unemployed; deferred earnings.
Refresher	5	To give advanced training on assessment, callers, visiting, and to discuss specialist problems so far as is appropriate to clerical officers, in liability of relatives, prevention of abuse, overpayments and voluntary unemployment.

subjects as assessment (of need and resources) over a wide range of situations; fraud; problems of unemployment; liability of reelatives; the prevention of abuse and overpayments. Instruction is also given on the duties of other social srvices and guidance given on ensuring co-operation with these services'.

Following the thirteen weeks' training period the Executive Officer is established for work but after three months of further local office experience he receives one further week's course. During that week he will be 'considering in greater depth problems arising in such fields as fraud, liability of relatives and unemployment, the further analysis of interviewing techniques, including discussion of observation training for the detection of abuse and welfare needs'. (*Fisher Report*, page 185.)

Clerical Officers receive a training along similar lines but restricted to three weeks only.

The full list of courses available at the two training centres at Billingham and Hinchley Wood for executive and clerical officers (reproduced on pp. 90 & 91) fails to mention any psychiatric or social work training, and yet it is emphasized repeatedly in the Fisher Committee report that staff need to understand claimants' behaviour and problems as well as to check abuse and assess correctly the needs of their clients. As can be seen from the list, great emphasis is placed upon training to deal with fraud, voluntary unemployment and overpayments. Liable relative specialists aim to cover 'the technical and legal aspect of their duty; recovery from liable relatives; fictitious desertion and undisclosed cohabitation; interviewing; dealing with the courts'. No mention is made in the 'Aims of Courses' of the social side of the job which must surely be delicate and require considerable human understanding and skills.

We have then a situation where a claimant suffering from chronic depression is interviewed by a clerk untrained to diagnose such a complaint. The interview is likely to be undertaken under pressure; quite possibly by a member of staff with little or no experience to compensate for the lack of training. A few vague questions are asked about previous gaps in employment and whether or not the claiment is 'disabled' before a decision is made to limit benefit to four weeks.

The communication gap

The defence of the Supplementary Benefits Commission against allegations that people are wrongly deprived of benefit has always been that men may renew their claim at the end of four weeks. At that stage a special interview will be arranged and the full circumstances of the individual investigated. In November 1971 a new form was introduced (B.663) which explained the need to renew the claim after four weeks. This is reproduced on the following page.

Department of Health and Social Security
Supplementary Allowance to Unemployed Claimant

Arrangements are being made with the Employment Exchange for payments to be made to you for a limited period while you look for a suitable job. In this area there are good openings for people under the age of 45 and we think you ought to be able to find work within the next four weeks.

You should look for work yourself as well as through the Employment Exchange, for example, by watching the advertisements in the local papers.

We hope you will find a suitable job without difficulty. If you experience any particular difficulty, we should like to know about this.

If you are still unemployed at the end of four weeks, you can renew your claim for supplementary benefit, and you will then be specially interviewed. Unless there are good reasons why you cannot find suitable work, your allowance might be stopped at that time. If this were done, you would be able to appeal against such a decision to an Appeal Tribunal.

Since that date the staff of social security offices have been instructed 'to issue form B.663 to every person whose supplementary allowance is limited under the four week rule, and every effort is made to see that this is done' (*Hansard*, 7.11.73). Paragraph four of this form includes the statement that 'if you are still unemployed at the end of four weeks, you can renew your claim for supplementary benefit, and you will then be specially interviewed'. It would seem then that every four week rule victim is carefully advised of his rights so that full safeguards against errors exist. In this context it seems remarkable that of the claimants in our survey unemployed in 1972 (after form B.663 was introduced), fully four-fifths were unaware that they could renew their claim at the end of the four week period if they remained unemployed when their benefit was cut. These men were under the impression that there was no hope of any further help after the four week period. Only ten of the fifty-six claimants in 1972 were aware of being informed of their right to renew their claim. Of course some may have received the leaflet and either read it and forgotten about it or failed to read it altogether. Whatever the explanation for the misunderstanding about the ability to renew a claim, the fact is that individuals are unaware of their rights.

Is this intentional or not? Do officers make it clear to claimants at the initial interview that the four week allowance may be renewed if for any reason the claimant remains out of work at the end of the four week period?

When claimants are not informed or misinformed

Implied at outset of claim that claimant could renew claim after four weeks	19
Told benefit would be for four weeks. No further information	49
Specifically told he would receive nothing after four weeks or told not to return to the office after four weeks	10
No warning. Benefit cut after about four weeks	8
Subjected to other forms of pressure	12
Total	98

In fifty-seven cases therefore it seems that the main problem has been a *lack* of information rather than misleading information. It is quite conceivable that this has occurred due to the severe strain under which the staff have been working in recent years. It is less easy to explain the 22 per cent or so of the sample who were either told specifically at the outset of their claim that no further benefit would be forthcoming at the end of the four week period or alternatively were subjected to other forms of pressure (e.g. to take a less skilled job).

A typical comment of this group was 'it was made perfectly clear either I find a job within four weeks or I starve'. It seems that the policeman role was paramount in these 20 per cent of cases. Equally disturbing was the indifferent approach to the 'special interviews' at the end of the four week period. We have already discussed in an earlier chapter the failure to recognize or to find out about medical disorders of the claimant even at the special interview after the four week period. But equally relevant is the failure to continue paying benefit to skilled men or ex-prisoners despite renewal of the claim when we are led to believe that all aspects of the case are fully discussed. Just how thorough is the special interview therefore? Of the sixteen unsuccessful applicants for a renewal of benefit three had severe mental problems, four were skilled or professional men, two had a criminal history and at least six out of the remaining seven had done all they reasonably could do to find a suitable job.

The search for work

One young man explained that he had applied for so many jobs that he couldn't remember most of them, but that on at least one occasion he had walked thirteen miles to a firm only to find there were no vacancies; another was studying car maintenance at night school in order to become a mechanic because 'there are jobs available for mechanics'; another said he had walked round to some eighty or ninety firms looking for labouring jobs without success; another complained of blisters on his feet caused by the endless walk in search for jobs; yet another accepted a job with a wage of £10 a week, fully £15 a week *below* his previous wage, because 'it was better than nothing'; and finally a young Jamaican simply explained that he goes down every day to the labour exchange, but they just say 'sorry, Mr X, there is just nothing in your line of job that we can offer you'.

We emphasize that despite this information available at the special interview every one of the claimants referred to was refused any further benefit. On the other hand, those who claimed successfully for an extension of benefit constitute an almost identical group in terms of incidence of illness, the proportion of skilled men and the proportion of ex-prisoners within the group.

We have, then, to conclude that an extension of benefit is no more likely to be given to sick men than to able-bodied men; no more likely to be given to ex-prisoners than to men with no criminal history and no more likely to be given to a skilled man than an unskilled man.

What is the rationale behind the decisions of the Supplementary Benefits Commission? As already pointed out, professional men with a degree behind them are more likely to reapply for benefit and more likely to succeed in obtaining an extension of benefit. But it appears that the success of these men is *not* a result of Supplementary Benefits Commission policy to allow twelve weeks benefit to professional or skilled men before applying the four week rule, but rather is due to the determination of these men to discover what their rights are and to demand that they be met in full. As one man explained: 'I said I was in the professional register; we had a set to and then everything was all right'.

The significance of office attitudes

The conclusion drawn from the evidence of special interviews at the end of the four week period is that individual office attitude may have more to do with the success of an applicant in obtaining an extension of benefit than have the qualifications of the claimant applying for an extension of benefit. If an officer is working in a sympathetic and understanding atmosphere, he will tend to take seriously the declaration of a claimant that he is unable to find work; will be more likely to be trusted and therefore to be informed of mental problems; and will tend to regard a criminal background as a drawback to the claimant in his efforts to find work rather than a reason for suspecting the worst and withdrawing benefit. On the other hand, an officer working in a 'hard' office will tend to demand written proof of applications for jobs; will tend to brush aside mental problems or drug-taking and tell the claimant to pull himself together and to settle down. Such an approach discourages an open discussion of medical problems or social problems generally and leads to the kind of misunderstandings and failures in communication referred to throughout this study.

The offices at which our sample of men had claimed benefit may be divided into almost distinct groups – those which tended to grant an extension of benefit if the claimant reapplied after four weeks; and those which did not.

There is very little overlap between the two groups of offices.

If we take an office which scored badly on the 'unsuccessful' reclaim scale (office W) a consistent policy emerges – that officers should not pay any money after the four week period unless the claimant has children, and even then officials should make life as unpleasant as possible for the claimant.

Seven of our respondents were office 'W' claimants and not one of them received understanding or sympathetic treatment. Only one claimant received benefit throughout an extended period of unemployment. He was married at the time with a baby. Nevertheless he was not only threatened with the four week rule, but also with prosecution and the demand to appear before a tribunal. None of these threats were carried out, and the claimant (a graduate) was remarkably understanding of the officials' approach. 'I couldn't have been trying any harder than I was to find a job, but I thought it only fair they should give me a nudge – after all, it's public funds'. Other claimants were less generous in their attitudes to supplementary benefit officials perhaps because for them the threats became reality. Three reapplied unsuccessfully for an extension of benefit despite having the right to an extension on grounds of ill-health or the possession of a skill. The remainder didn't go to the trouble of reapplying or obtained just one additional week's benefit to fill the gap until a *smaller* amount of unemployment benefit became payable.

At the other end of the spectrum is an office with what appears to be a wholly positive attitude towards claimants – 'F' – at which five of our claimants had received supplementary allowances. All five had been granted extensions of benefit beyond the four week period – one without reapplication, having explained at the initial interview that he was under treatment for a nervous breakdown after a long psychiatric history; and the remaining four after reapplication. All four men who returned to the office to enquire about renewal of benefit were physically and mentally fit and reapplied on what appeared to be genuine grounds of inability to find suitable employment within the four week period. Two of the men were unskilled and although quite clearly both were seeking work, it is not possible to point to any factors distinguishing these men from the unsuccessful applicants for extensions of benefit at other offices. Indeed in many cases at other offices sick and skilled men were denied any extension when these factors alone qualified them for longer periods of full benefit.

Rather than suggesting that the staff in the 'W' office are themselves less generous and understanding than those in the South Eastern office, it is almost certainly the case that the pressure of work and level of demands on the North Western office were considerably greater during the period under review than they were in the South East. Unemployment was at more than twice the level in the former than the latter area, and although allowance must be made by the Supplementary Benefits Commission for the numbers of men unemployed in different areas, nevertheless it can be expected that greater concern about the need to economize would be felt in areas of high unemployment where the spending of public money seemed excessive.

Economics more important than need?

The findings in these two offices are confirmed by an examination of all the offices included in the study. Although the study is too small to permit firm conclusions, the findings do suggest that in the South West and Midlands with intermediate levels of unemployment, a more lenient approach by interviewing officers is permitted than in the North West. In London and the South Eastern areas in general, officers are able to provide a service most closely approximating to the official policy of the Supplementary Benefits Commission. The conflict between the two roles of offices (the welfare role and the police role) can be expected to increase in any office as the local level of demand for benefits increases with the unemployment level and to decrease as the demand for funds and unemployment levels fall. Contrary to this tendency, of course, a more lenient approach is needed in areas of high unemployment. We have, then, a situation in which the health, skills and circumstances of the claimant seem to be less important in determining the treatment he receives from supplementary benefit officers than the policy of the office at the time of the claim. Furthermore it appears that the office policy would appear to vary inversely with the employment situation – a more generous policy being implemented in areas with the least employment problems and vice-versa.

The conflict of motives

But a more fundamental fault than the pressure of work, which could at least in theory be eliminated, is the conflict of motives of supplementary benefit officials inherent in the instructions of the Supplementary Benefits Commission. *The Report of the Committee on Abuse of Social Security Benefits* (H.M.S.O., Cmnd. 5228, paragraph 32) draws attention to the conflict between 'measures taken to prevent and detect abuse' and 'prompt and sympathetic dealing with claims'. The Report points out that the obligation to deal promptly and sympathetically with claims is inherent in the aims of the social security scheme. And yet how can an official be sympathetic with a claimant if he is carefully assessing the possibility that the claimant is making a fraudulent application for benefit, or if he suspects that the claimant is unwilling to work and therefore doesn't deserve any help?

The two roles of policeman and welfare officer must surely be separated rather than combined in the same officers if either of the conflicting goals is to be satisfactorily achieved.

The third element of the conflict faced by supplementary benefit officials is the need to economize in the use of public funds. This requirement reinforces the role of policeman in that when applying the four week rule, if a claimant can be labelled 'workshy' and denied benefit after four weeks, this saves the Commission's resources. But the need for economy provides a powerful incentive to officials to conceal information vital to claimants if they are to receive their full rights. It therefore may interfere with the treatment of claimants accepted by the officials as genuine. We have already referred to the form B.663 which is, according to the Minister, sent to every four week rule claimant to inform him of the right to renew his claim for benefit at the end of the four week period. If the form is handed to a claimant with a careful verbal explanation of his right to reapply, then any claimant with a genuine case would return to the office after four weeks. For the official this would mean that an investigation should be made of the circumstances of the individual. If, for instance, he claims that he is a drug addict and unable to cope with a job, then medical reports will be needed and these may recommend that benefits continue to be paid for an indefinite period until the claimant solves his drug problems. This may not be achieved, as one claimant explained, even after three hospital 'cures' lasting in at least one case for a full year. If an official is instructed to economize in the use of public funds, should he tell the drug addict to pull himself together and not to return to the office for money after a period of four weeks? Or alternatively should he provide the long-term financial security needed by the addict, at considerable public expense? The conflict in the official's mind is obvious. The criticism of the four week rule is that it puts the boot all too firmly on the official's foot – a few sharp words and a 'lost' form B.663 in many cases ensures that a claimant's file can be closed. And why should an overworked official worry about the social consequences? He will probably never know that his claimant resorted to stealing food, money or drugs.

Claimants under stress

Working under pressure, often with little experience of the issues and problems likely to arise, can lead to unexpected trouble in a supplementary benefit office where claimants have, at times, violent temperaments or mental problems exacerbated or perhaps created by their desperate financial circumstances. A claimant in Keighley gives us an insight into the tensions and emotions sometimes created by the decision of an official. The claimant had been forced to leave a recent job on a building site after a fight which caused his 'opponent' to spend nine weeks in hospital! He admitted to having a fiery temper and explained that he reared up at the unsuspecting clerk who told him his benefit had been stopped.

'It was sheer anger', he explained. 'I nearly got put into jail for it – it was capitalist against a peasant. I tried to get a hold of him over the counter. I'm not used to being pushed around – I've done six years in the paratroopers and have paid taxes for years – they give you the idea it's coming out of their own pocket – I'm entitled to it. I've paid it in and not drawn a penny. I had a woman and child dependant on me. I wasn't bothered about myself – but I was bothered about her and the child. They just ignored me. I took evidence of applying for jobs. I got building sites to write on a piece of paper that there was no work there. I felt the anger I used to feel in Egypt and Cyprus – I killed men there and I felt the same – so angry I could have killed anyone who came to the door. I did everything possible to find a job – even wrote away to the oil rigs and things, but nothing was forthcoming. I even tried to get into the Merchant Navy and the Army again, but I'd had a medical discharge so I couldn't get in again. I used to walk the floor worrying at night.'

No doubt the clerk concerned was under the impression that jobs were available in the area. But the claimant was genuine enough when describing his bitter resentment at the 'unjust' withdrawal of his benefit. The problem in this case and a number of others would seem to be that unskilled men are offered no choice at all about the jobs they must accept. The ex-paratrooper applied almost exclusively for building jobs and expressed a wish to work outside, having always done so (though he had applied for one factory job which had already been taken). If the Supplementary Benefits Commission expects such a man to accept a job peeling potatoes or wiping coffee tables in a restaurant they will almost certainly stretch the tolerance of human nature beyond endurance. It is surely important to take into account the expectations and aspirations of unskilled as well as skilled claimants. The view that claimants are treated 'like cattle' expresses the feelings so often repeated by the men interviewed for this study. A semi-skilled laboratory assistant has different aspirations from an unskilled building labourer and both these men differ in their expectations from an ex-kitchen porter.

For every one client who displays some violent emotions towards the official or clerk interviewing him, there are many others who feel anger and bitterness towards a system they see as unjust. Two-thirds of our sample felt that it had been unfair to grant benefit for only four weeks, and the reasons given for their point of view are worth noting.

The failure of officials to take personal circumstances into account was a complaint more often expressed than any other. But a number of claimants pointed out that jobs were not available locally and in these circumstances four weeks was not enough time for men to find work. Others pointed to the apparent inconsistency of giving benefit to some men for months and to others for only a few weeks. This kind of criticism is inevitable of a system shrouded in secrecy when officials have a substantial element of discretion, and when the rights of claimants are not clearly and unambiguously stated. Resentment was also caused by the feeling that after paying taxes and stamps while at work, a full benefit should be paid until suitable work was available.

The resentments were largely justified in that they resulted almost exclusively from misapplications of the rule or unduly harsh interpretations of the discretionary powers available to officials. A claimant needs an inordinately passive temperament to remain calm when deprived of his only source of income if he feels, often rightly, that his personal circumstances render that deprivation unjust and perhaps illegal.

Appeals

It might be argued that the right of appeal against withdrawal of benefit (or against a number of other decisions of the S.B.C.) provided an adequate safeguard against wrongful decisions by individual officers. The Handbook points out that if a claimant appeals, then he will continue to receive an allowance (albeit a reduced one) until his appeal is heard within about four weeks. If a man is deprived of benefit when he genuinely cannot find work, then the appeal procedure is open to him. How does this 'safeguard' work out in practice?

Of the entire sample only three men appealed against the withdrawal of benefit, and all unsuccessfully, although fully forty-eight were without benefit after four weeks and unable to find a job. Only ten of those concerned were aware that they could appeal, and of these, seven failed to do so either because they felt they had no chance of winning: 'I'd have got shot down – I'm a peasant'; or because they did not know how to set about an appeal or alternatively because they were 'sick and tired of it all'. The evidence from this study suggests that claimants are not encouraged to appeal against decisions and are not automatically informed of their right to do so or given the necessary information about procedure. The attitude of claimants to appeals was probably most cogently put by one who said 'appeals are a laugh – it's like a copper arresting a copper'. Certainly the experience of the three men who did appeal supports this view. To take just one example, a claimant under treatment for a nervous break-down, and who was represented at his appeal by two welfare officers and three Claimants Union members, had his appeal rejected on the grounds that he should obtain an Army Pension. The Army Pension was eventually paid after an eight-month struggle by the welfare department, but in the meantime the supplementary benefits office failed to accept responsibility for this claimant and the Appeal Tribunal failed to reverse the decision of the official concerned.

7 The National Implications

From October 1968 to March 1973 the four week rule was applied to 275 000 men all over Britain. If we assume that our sample of ninety-eight men drawn from areas in the North, Midlands, South and West of Britain is representative of all four week rule cases, then we can estimate the numbers of men who have been deprived of benefit whilst still unemployed; the numbers of sick men deprived of benefit and the numbers of men either with a criminal history or driven to crime by the destitution following withdrawal of benefit.

53 per cent of our sample remained unemployed at the end of the four week period and either failed to reapply for benefit or reapplied unsuccessfully. In national terms the results of this survey suggest that:

1. Since 1968 about 137 000 men have been deprived of benefit after four weeks despite remaining unemployed at that time.

2. 55 000 mentally or physically ill claimants have been deprived of benefit after four weeks despite being out of work at the time.

3. 25 000 men with a criminal history have been driven back by the four week rule to the one 'solution' they know – thieving.

4. Some 27 500 men who have been subjected to the four week rule since 1968, have resorted to crime for the first time in their lives during the weeks following withdrawal of benefit.

5. 88 000 men probably had no income whatsoever when their benefit was withdrawn.

6. A further 49 000 men probably had only a small amount

of unemployment benefit each week, but insufficient to live on and in many cases not even enough to pay the rent.

In contrast to the staggering figure of first offenders amongst four week rule victims given above, it appears that the numbers of men who reclaim benefit successfully and who resort to crime for the first time are very small. In our sample, for instance, only one claimant who successfully reapplied for benefit resorted to crime. He was suffering from a chronic anxiety disorder and sold the drugs he received from the doctor as well as doing a bit of shop-lifting to supplement his benefit. We cannot generalize from one case. However the fact that the four week rule has probably been responsible for some 27 500 cases of petty thieving or other minor offences since 1968 is striking enough.

Since the accuracy of these conclusions about the overall national impact of the four week rule depends on the representativeness of our sample, the methods used to obtain the sample will be described in some detail in Appendix 3. It should be mentioned here, however, that nearly four fifths of the sample were first contacted outside the employment exchange while the remaining one fifth were interviewed as a result of 6325 house to house contacts. The sample is, therefore, inevitably biased towards those frequently unemployed or unemployed over a long period. However, these men form the majority of unemployed single men registered at employment exchanges at any one point in time and any bias in the national implications of the four week rule, discussed above, can be expected to be relatively small. In particular the effects of the rule upon the incidence of crime may well be *under*-estimated since those with a criminal record might be expected to number heavily amongst the 'refusals' for interview.

8 Conclusions and Recommendations

The Supplementary Benefits Commission is responsible for the livelihood of some six million people (including dependants) at any one time and this study has concentrated upon a small section of this dependent group in the hope of illustrating just how complex the situations of each individual claimant usually are; and just how much in need of help rather than punishment and deprivation are many of the people so often branded as scroungers and layabouts. We cannot dismiss as inevitable the fact that some 55 000 mentally or physically sick men have been deprived of benefit since 1968 on the assumption that they are not making adequate efforts to find work. We cannot ignore the fact that some 27 500 men have been driven to commit petty criminal offences by a too-hasty decision to withdraw benefit. Nor can we accept the shifting of the burden of unemployment from the State to mothers (in many cases widowed or separated mothers), flat-sharers or landladies – whoever in fact is available to take on the responsibilities of a man unable to find work when the State withdraws its assistance.

Who or what is to blame for the failure of the system of support for the unemployed and sick? Surely not the officials manning the counters of supplementary benefit offices. These men and women merely have the unpleasant task of trying to operate an inoperable system. The fault lies in the piecemeal and inadequate system of social security which has developed over the past thirty years or so: the fact that the basic national insurance pension remains below susbsistence level, leaving the S.B.C. to make up the difference; the fact that no comprehensive disability allowance is available, leaving the S.B.C. to finance a substantial proportion of the disabled; the fact that unsupported mothers, with the exception of widows are, more often than not, dependent upon the S.B.C. either for the whole or a part of their income; the fact that the flat-rate unemployment and sickness benefit levels remain below subsistence level, leaving the S.B.C. to make up the difference for this further group.

Beveridge in 1945 envisaged the national insurance schemes as providing all these groups with an adequate income, with the exception of a small proportion who for special reasons slipped through the net. In the 1970s we are no further forward towards putting into practice the Beveridge principle than we were in 1945. A series of reforms will be discussed below which are not only necessary in themselves if some of the worst pockets of poverty in Britain today are to be eliminated, but which would also achieve our objective of reducing significantly the work-load of the S.B.C. so that the nature of the service provided by the offices could be radically altered.

Our recommendations can be divided into three distinct parts:

1. The abolition of the four week rule. (The amendment to the rule, introduced since this book was written, is discussed in the Preface.)

2 The extension and rationalization of a number of national insurance and other benefits.

3. The reorganization of the Supplementary Benefits Commission.

The abolition of the four week rule

The justification for such a policy rests on four basic conclusions of this study:

(a) that about 98 per cent of claimants wish to work all or more of the time so that the rule is unnecessary. This conclusion is supported by the most thorough official investigation ever undertaken of voluntary unemployment which indicated that only 2·3 per cent of the long-term unemployed had lost the will to work. Further evidence of the desire to work was the widespread incidence of depression, sleeplessness, and a number of other symptoms during unemployment.

(b) That substantial controls against voluntary unemployment exist in addition to the four week rule so that the latter, which is anyway a very drastic expedient, is superfluous.

(c) The operation of the four week rule gives rise to a number of undesirable social effects.

(d) The four week rule appears to urge only 5 per cent of claimants back into suitable jobs somewhat earlier than they might otherwise have returned to work, and the financial cost to the other 95 per cent far outweighs the limited economic gain in this very small minority of cases.

(e) The removal of the four week rule would also, desirably in my view, undermine those other functions which the rule at present surreptitiously performs:

  (i) By pushing men into lower-paid, lower-status jobs than they would otherwise voluntarily accept, it helps to make a low-wage economy work.

 (ii) By reinforcing prejudices about scrounging, it distracts attention from the vastly greater problem of the Welfare State today in the form of massive unmet need.

(iii) By assuming unemployment among single unskilled men reflects laziness or moral failure, it emphasizes an authoritarian approach to economic problems and strengthens class divisions within society.

The extension and rationalization of a number of national insurance and other benefits

The Sick and Disabled

Fully 459 000 sick and disabled persons were drawing supplementary benefits in October 1973 (*Hansard,* Parliamentary Answers 25.10.73), representing some 30 per cent of persons categorized as 'impaired'. The consequences for the unemployed of the pressure of work and confusion of aims of supplementary benefit officials have already been discussed, but the situation is similarly unsatisfactory for the disabled for whom under-assessment of benefit and the failure to grant exceptional needs grants and allowances can lead to very real hardship.

In order to discover why so many disabled people have to

rely on supplementary benefits, we need to look at the piece-meal and inconsistent provisions for disabled people. If for instance a man was disabled during the War or at work, he will probably be covered by the war and industrial injury schemes. On the other hand another with perhaps equal or more severe disabilities suffered since birth may receive no benefits as of right at all. Similarly many disabled housewives and children have no rights to benefit. The Rowntree Trust has been commissioned to distribute a relatively small sum to severely congenitally handicapped children; and of course thalidomide children have been awarded substantial sums of compensation by the Distillers Company. At the same time other equally severely handicapped children are receiving nothing because the necessary pressure has not yet been exerted upon the Government.

The Labour Government is tackling a number of these problems in the 1974/5 session, but what is needed is a *comprehensive* policy covering all disabled people regardless of the cause of the disability. Secondly the benefits must vary according to the degree of capacity. The more disabled a person is, the less he is likely to be able to earn and the more benefit he will need. Benefits based on an individual contribution record are therefore inappropriate for the disabled since some people never have the opportunity to contribute to a national insurance scheme and should not be penalized for a lifelong incapacity.

Any comprehensive disability allowance would result in substantial savings in supplementary benefits, and Professor Peter Townsend estimates (*The Times,* 10.12.73) that the cost of such allowances comparable with the industrial injury and war disablement pensions would be in the region of £170m a year. A further £50m might be spent extending national insurance benefits to all disabled persons who have contributed to the scheme to be paid in addition to the flat-rate benefit; thirdly £25m might be spent on earnings-related supplements to ease the drop in standard of living of relatively highly paid persons who are suddenly disabled; and finally £50m would be needed for dietary and other special payments.

Expenditure of about £300m would cover all these items, but with £200m a year a basic flat-rate allowance of £12·80 per week (at 1973 prices) at the 100 per cent rate (for the severely disabled) and some additional special payments could be made, removing the vast majority of disabled people from the books of supplementary benefit offices, and providing an independent income based for the first time on the degree of disability.

Old Age Pensioners

A total of 2 149 000 pensioners (about 30 per cent) are receiving supplementary pensions in 1973 for two reasons:

(a) the flat-rate pension is below subsistence level to the extent of about £2 per week in the case of a single pensioner and rather more in the case of a married couple;

(b) occupational pension schemes cover only 52·6 per cent of male manual workers, and of all pensioners receiving occupational pensions 40 per cent were receiving less than £2 per week.

An increase in the national insurance pension by £2 for a single person and by £2·75 for a married couple would enable nearly one million pensioners to cease drawing a supplementary pension. The cost of such an increase in the pension would be in the region of £500m when the savings in supplementary pensions and some tax clawback are taken into account. Not only would such a reform provide independence for a million pensioners, but it would ensure a subsistence income for the half million or more old people now living on a basic pension below supplementary benefit level and yet refusing to accept State charity. Needless to say these increases represent an absolute minimum which needs to be provided urgently (in addition to the Labour Government's recent increases) and does not in any way represent an adequate solution to the problem of poverty in old age. The needs of the elderly are in some respects (e.g. heating and diet) greater than those of the younger age groups. A subsistence level income for a married couple aged, say, forty may therefore be inadequate for a couple in their seventies.

Single, separated and divorced mothers

A third group which could and should be freed from dependence upon supplementary benefits are the ¼m single, separated and divorced mothers who now draw benefit. At present widowed mothers are treated considerably more generously by the State than any other unsupported mother. A widowed mother receives a basic allowance as of right of £10·00 plus allowances of about £4 for each child (high for the first child and declining for second, third and subsequent children). These allowances are regarded as a substitute for the dead father's income and are not therefore withdrawn if the mother works. The vast majority of widows are therefore able to live without resort to supplementary benefits. In 1968 only 12 per cent of widowed mothers depended on supplementary benefits.

In contrast to the situation of widowed mothers, the position of single, separated and divorced mothers depends very much on the ability and willingness of the father to contribute maintenance payments above the poverty line. Very few men are able, whether or not they are willing, to maintain two households at a reasonable standard of living. The result is that some 64 per cent of single, separated and divorced mothers depend upon supplementary benefits, or some half a million such families. These women also have little or no incentive to work because if they earn more than £2 per week, their supplementary benefit is withdrawn pound for pound in line with earnings. For a number of reasons (primarily the very low wages still offered to women and the costs of working – of travel, clothing and food away from home) unsupported mothers find it impossible to raise the standard of living of their families above the poverty (or supplementary benefit) level.

We would argue that families already penalized by the loss of a father should not be condemned to a life of poverty. For social as well as administrative reasons, therefore, it is very much hoped that the Finer Committee's recommendation of an allowance for unsupported mothers will be implemented without unnecessary delay. The introduction of an allowance at the same level as that for widowed mothers would cost £200m or less when the substantial savings in supplementary benefit payments are taken into account. Some hope of adding a few luxuries like simple holidays and fruit and good meat to the basic essentials of life could thus be provided for this hard-pressed group, and at the same time, from the administrative point of view, the great majority of unsupported mothers could be removed from the supplementary benefit files.

Even after an expenditure of some £900m, however, fully 3¼m people would remain dependent upon supplementary allowances or pensions. The 3¼m residual claimants fall into the following three groups:

1. About 1m pensioners who, due to cost considerations, cannot immediately be lifted out of the poverty level.

2. About 1m unemployed persons.

3. About 1¼m widowed, divorced or separated women without children.

Unemployed persons

A reduction in the numbers of unemployed persons depending upon supplementary benefits could be achieved by an increase in the flat-rate unemployment and sickness benefits by £2 per week for a single person and by £2·75p per week for married couples; and at the same time an increase and extension of family allowances to £2 for each child including the first. The cost of both these reforms together would be in the region of £650m (Parliamentary Answer, 14.11.73, *Hansard*), taking into account the substantial Exchequer gains from the concurrent elimination of child tax allowances and the savings in supplementary benefit payments.

Widowed, divorced or separated women without children

One and a quarter million women are included in this group of supplementary benefit claimants, and it can be argued that their dependence upon the State reflects not only the failure of our national insurance system, but also the very real financial disadvantages to women of their traditional role as keeper of the home.

A particularly tragic section of single women without children for whom some specific assistance is needed are those who give up their careers in order to care for an elderly or disabled relative. The National Council for the Single Woman and her Dependants estimates that some 250 000 single women are involved. No payment is made to these women for the services they provide, and yet an elderly or disabled person who might otherwise be forced into hospital would cost the State at least £13 per week. At the very least, unemployment benefit should be available to this group and national insurance contributions should be credited to them so that when the disabled or elderly relative dies or is finally admitted to hospital, the caring person can draw an income until she is able to work. So often, when freed from their responsibilities, these women are too old to return to paid work, having lost income, pension rights, promotion prospects and sometimes savings.

The Labour Party proposal to introduce compulsory earnings-related national insurance contributions for working women will go some way towards enabling widowed, divorced and separated women to become self-sufficient. Serious consideration should also be given to the possibility of crediting women with contributions while they remain at home during the years of child-rearing. Such a step might make possible the elimination of the married pension and its substitution by single pensions for men and women whether married or single based upon the individual's actual or credited contributions.

The introduction of a comprehensive national insurance policy along the lines outlined above would provide security and independence for the bulk of men and women now drawing supplementary benefits. The original concept of the National Assistance Board (now called the Supplementary Benefits Commission) as the agency of last resort catering for the small minority of persons not covered by the national insurance schemes could then be restored.

The Supplementary Benefits Commission transformed

It is envisaged, then, that the number of claimants at supplementary benefit offices could be reduced to 1–2m at any one time, and eventually the numbers could fall well below this as funds become available for a steadily increasing pension and as the opportunities and pay of women conform more closely to those of men. At such time a specialist service could be provided by officers trained to assist ex-prisoners, new immigrants, ex-hospital patients and other minority groups who for any reason have little or no contribution record and who may need guidance about training and job opportunities. The image of the office would be that of a social work department and one would hope for a relationship between officer and claimant similar to that between a good social worker and her families.

It might be argued that the shift of the majority of claimants from supplementary benefit offices to national insurance offices would merely shift the burden of the workshy from one office to another. If, however, the evidence of this study is accepted that the loss of the desire to work is closely related to a total rejection of the established values of society and therefore likely to be accompanied by criminal activities, or alternatively is a symptom of depression or other mental disturbances, then there is no reason to expect people normally at work and with a full contribution record to remain out of work for longer than necessary. The national insurance and disability benefits office would therefore be involved in simple financial transactions in accordance with the legally defined rights of the individuals concerned, depending largely on giro orders and brief office interviews during which the facts of the case would be established. Those needing more careful and considered interviews and follow-up work would be confined to supplementary benefit offices with trained specialist staff operating on a social work basis whilst ensuring adequate financial provision for their clients.

What will it all cost?

Approximately £1500m at 1973 rates would be needed to achieve the initial objectives which can be summarized as follows:

1. To provide a disability allowance for all disabled people pitched according to disability but at a rate of £12·80 for a person with a 100 per cent disability and at proportionately reducing rates for those with less severe disabilities.

2. To provide subsistence level pensions for all those with full national insurance contribution records and average or below average rent levels.

3. To provide an unsupported mothers' allowance comparable with the widowed mothers' allowance.

4. To increase unemployment and sickness benefit to subsistence levels for single persons and married couples.

5. To extend family allowances to the first child and to increase them to £2 per child.

The figure of £1500m seems excessive at first glance, but this needs to be considered in the context of the Conservative Government's Tax Credit proposals. These tax reforms would cost fully £1300m and would benefit all households to the extent of about £3 per week with the exception of groups left out of the scheme, notably supplementary benefit recipients including, as we have already noted, many disabled people, unsupported mothers and sick and unemployed people. In contrast, the benefit of the reforms costing £1500m would be concentrated very heavily on the most deprived sections of the community, at the same time making possible a radical transformation of the Supplementary Benefits Commission and an entirely new approach to a sharply diminished problem of poverty. In that context the four week rule, which owes its origin to political and administrative conditions which would then have ceased to exist, would naturally lapse into abeyance as a relic of an earlier stage of the Welfare State which would then have been surpassed.

Postscript

Four weeks after a copy of this study was made available to the Department of Health and Social Security, an announcement was made to the effect that the four week rule was to be amended. In place of the automatic withdrawal of benefit at the end of a four week period *unless* a claimant re-applies for benefit, the procedure in future will allow for an interview with an Unemployment Review Officer before benefit is withdrawn. Although in theory this procedure represents an improvement upon that described in the preceding pages, the effects upon claimants are likely to remain largely unchanged for the following reasons:

1. The conflicting motives of the Supplementary Benefits Commission remain unchanged.

2. The shortage of staff and the inappropriate working conditions remain unchanged. (The Commission in a letter to the Child Poverty Action Group admitted a need to increase the number of Unemployment Review Officers but did not indicate that such an increase would be implemented.)

3. The criteria for deciding whether or not a claimant is fit for work remain unchanged.

4. The definition of a 'skilled man' remains ambiguous.

5. The training of Unemployment Review Officers continues to neglect the fact that much of the work concerns people with psychological or emotional difficulties.

6. Decisions concerning the availability of work in any area will continue to be made at the discretion of officers from the Supplementary Benefits Commission and Department of Employment.

The reforms outlined in Chapter 8 remain necessary if the experiences described in this book are not to be repeated.

Appendix 1

The Four Week Rule Defined (extract from the *Supplementary Benefits Handbook*)

The first two (controls) apply to persons under the age of forty-five who are free from any serious physical disability and who have shown no signs of mental disorder or instability.

The first relates to fit men who are single, unskilled and under age forty-five. In areas where it has been agreed with the Department of Employment and Productivity that the arrangements shall apply, because work is available of an unskilled nature, e.g. as a labourer, kitchen porter or garage attendant, every new or repeat claim by such a man comes within the control. Instead of being given an allowance of unlimited duration, he is at the outset given one for four weeks only, and is told that he should be able to find work within four weeks, and will be expected to do so, and that the Commission might refuse further benefit after that period. At this early stage of a claim, labouring work or portering is not of course regarded as suitable for a man who has a special skill such as a trained craftsman.

If at the end of four weeks a man is still out of work and suitable work is no longer available, or for other reasons it is clear that he remains unemployed through no fault of his own, the allowance is continued for whatever period is appropriate. If suitable work is available, the allowance ceases and the man is told that he can, if he wishes, appeal against the cessation of the allowance to the Appeal Tribunal (paragraphs 211–218). If he appeals, the allowance is continued at an interim level (normally twenty shillings less than the rate otherwise payable) until the appeal has been heard. If the decision is in the claimant's favour, the allowance continues at the normal rate and the amount deducted pending the appeal hearing is made up.

The second control comes into operation only if an allowance to someone required to register for work has lasted for three months. It relates to all other fit men under the age of forty-five, whether single or married, and to women under the age of forty-five. A claimant who has been drawing a supplementary allowance for about three months is asked to come to the local office for interview. This interview provides an opportunity for a full discussion with the claimant of his efforts to find work, of the additional steps he might take to find himself a job, of any difficulties which may be preventing him from doing so and of any ways in which he could be helped. If it is clear that he is not really trying to get a job, he is warned that he has a liability to maintain himself and his dependants, if any, and that his allowance cannot be continued indefinitely while he looks for the precise job he would like as opposed to the kind of job which may be available for him. If the interviewing officer's knowledge of suitable possibilities or the advice of the Employment Exchange suggests that the claimant could obtain employment if he made a little more effort to do so, then, *unless there are dependants to whom this would cause hardship,* he is told that his allowance will be continued for four weeks only and might not be renewed. If he is still unemployed at the end of four weeks, his allowance may be terminated: if this is done, he is told of his right of appeal to the Appeal Tribunal.

At the review interview, each individual claimant is considered in the light of his own particular problems about getting work. For example, a young person with a vocational diploma or degree, waiting for a job appropriate to his qualifications in circumstances in which it is likely that it will be some time before he could hope to be successful, might be advised in the meanwhile to take, say, a clerical job. Where an older man has lost a well-paid job, and events show that he is setting his sights too high, he will be helped to face the realities of his situation. Men with dependants and other men whose claims cause difficulty may be asked to discuss their problems with a member of the Advisory Committee panel (paragraph 224).

The third and fourth controls concern people who are not fully fit and all people over forty-five. Standard practice is to review all allowances at the end of about six months, except those for men aged sixty and over, which are reviewed after about a year. This differentiation takes account of the fact that age itself may well be the main handicap in getting a new job. Unemployment review specialists go through the records of the long-term unemployed and arrange for them to be specially interviewed. The interviews are designed to find out the underlying causes of unemployment, to help those who are handicapped by personal problems to solve them, to give practical help to those who have been losing heart in trying to find work and stimulate them to make further efforts, and to persuade those who do not want work that it is in their own interest to take it.

Appendix 2

The only piece of evidence in support of the public resentment of claimants was a report on 11 000 men, all unemployed for at least three months, which showed that, when called for interview, fully 60 per cent of the men ceased to draw allowances either before or soon after the interview, 'most found work for themselves; some were placed in work by the unemployment exchanges, and in a few cases of special difficulty some were found work by the unemployment review officers'. (Department of Health and Social Security, Report 1968.) The figures do on first sight suggest that some men may be too willing to rely on supplementary benefits. However the following questions would need to be answered before this conclusion was reached:–

1. What proportion of the 60 per cent who found work were forced to accept a job with a wage well below that in their previous job?

2. What proportion of the 60 per cent had mental or physical disabilities, as a result of which, although forced into work by the interviewer, the claimant soon became unemployed again?

3. What proportion of those unemployed for at least three months would be expected to find work in the period under consideration even if no interview took place?

4. What proportion of the men remained unemployed though ceasing to draw allowances?

In view of the available evidence that only a very small proportion of the unemployed are workshy, we would suggest that the great majority of those who ceased to claim before or after an interview would fall within the above four categories.

Appendix 3

The fieldwork for the study carried out by Social and Community Planning Research involved interviews with ninety-eight men who had been subjected to the four week rule. A contact questionnaire was used to establish whether a single man under the age of forty-five had been unemployed since July 1968 (when the four week rule was introduced) and, if so, whether he had been subjected to the four week rule. If he had been granted supplementary benefit and had been warned that he would receive it for only four weeks, he was defined as having been subjected to the four week rule and therefore as eligible for interview.

Sampling procedure

No list of those who have been subjected to the four week rule is available. Since they constitute a very small proportion of the overall population (slightly under one per cent of British adults), it was not feasible to find them by searching for them within a cross-section of the general population. Accordingly other methods had to be used.

Two methods were tried out in a small feasibility study.

The feasibility study

Lists of areas in which the four week rule was being applied (mainly areas of high employment) were supplied by DHSS. Five of these were selected in different parts of the country:

Keighley
Stoke-on-Trent
Crawley
Bristol
London (Shoreditch)

Interviewers spent five days in each area, two days outside the local employment exchange contacting men as they entered or left, and three days knocking on doors in a selection of working class streets in the neighbourhood of the exchange.

The contacts outside the employment exchanges produced per fieldwork day about three times the number who had been subjected to the four week rule as were found by knocking on doors. However, more of the eligible employment exchange contacts refused to be interviewed on the main questionnaire and the sample obtained by this method obviously contained a higher proportion of men who had been unemployed relatively frequently and for relatively long periods. In other words, a sample obtained by this method would under-represent those for whom, it could be argued, the four week rule worked most effectively in that they had obtained a job before the four week period was up. It was therefore decided that both methods would be used in the main survey.

The sampling frame for the main survey

Up-to-date lists of the areas in which the four week rule was being applied were again obtained from the DHSS. The rule had been suspended during the miners' strike in early 1972 and was gradually reintroduced from mid-April onwards. The lists supplied purported to include all those areas operating the four week rule at the beginning of August 1972.

On examination of this list, it was found to differ considerably from that supplied earlier in the year which had included all those areas operating the four week rule before its suspension at the time of the miners' strike. In particular, it contained a high proportion of small urban and rural areas, particularly in the South West and relatively few areas in the major conurbations. Since people were eligible for interview if they had had the four week rule applied at any time since July 1968, it was decided to combine the two lists into a composite sampling frame.

The areas on the list were arranged within the broad regional divisions used by DHSS, but the so-called London regions (London North, London West and London South included the whole of East and South East England; a separate Inner London region was therefore defined to ensure that these areas were adequately represented. Twenty-five areas were then selected, the number of people interviewed in each region being proportionate to the total number in the region on the master list.

Finding eligible respondents – door-to-door contacting

Maps were obtained for the districts surrounding the employment exchanges in the selected areas and, with the help of interviewers who inspected the areas, the working class residential streets were listed. Interviewers spent four fieldwork days in each area systematically knocking on doors to find out whether any single men under the age of forty-five lived there. Recalls were made if there was no contact at the address and much of the work was therefore carried out in the evening. When someone in the relevant category was found, the contact questionnaire was used to establish whether he had been subjected to the four week rule and was therefore eligible for interview on the long questionnaire.

Labour exchange contacting

Interviewers spent two fieldwork days outside the employment exchange in the area; they stopped men as they entered or left and checked whether they were single and under forty-five. If they were in this category, the contact questionnaire was used to establish whether they had had the four week rule applied during this or an earlier period of unemployment. If they proved to be eligible for the full interview, an appointment was made to see them, usually in their own home.

   This fieldwork took place between 26th September and the end of November 1972.

Success rate and appraisal of the sample

The fifty fieldwork days outside employment exchanges produced a number of contacts eligible for interview in line with expectations based on the feasibility study; 109 single men under the age of forty-five who had been subject to the four week rule were found and eighty of these were interviewed in full.

The 200 fieldwork days spent on door-to-door contact work had been expected from the feasibility study to produce 30–40 men eligible for interview; in this case, however, only about half the expected number of eligible contacts were achieved; twenty-two men who had been subjected to the four week rule were found and eighteen of them agreed to be interviewed.

The reasons for this lower contact rate are probably several. The feasibility study was on a small scale (five areas) and there may therefore have been a considerable degree of chance variation; in addition, the feasibility study was conducted mainly in large urban centres to which young single men may tend to graduate. The main study, on the other hand, included a number of small urban and rural centres. It also included more areas where unemployment was low. Door-to-door contacting was therefore likely to produce very few men who had been unemployed during the relevant period. Because the majority were contacted outside employment exchanges, the sample is inevitably biased towards those frequently unemployed or unemployed over a long period. The survey therefore cannot adequately appraise the effects for the application of the four week rule on those rarely unemployed and unemployed for short periods. However, the sample represents the hard core of unemployed single men who form the majority of those in this category registered at employment exchanges at any one point in time. They are almost certainly the ones whom the four week rule is particularly designed to influence since a large proportion of those in the relevant category who are infrequently unemployed and only for short periods are likely to be men with no employment problems.

Analysis of contacts and interviews achieved
Employment Exchanges (fifty fieldwork days)

Total number of single men under forty-five contacted   749
Not subject to four week rule since July 1968   640

Subject to four week rule and eligible for interview	109
Interviewed in full	80
Refused to give name or make appointment	16
Appointment made but not kept/false name and address given	18

Door-to-door contacting (200 fieldwork days)

Total number of addresses contacted	6325
Number of single men under forty-five contacted	605
Ineligible for interview:	
Not unemployed since July 1968	417
Not been subject to four week rule	175
Total ineligible	591

Eligible for interview (i.e. subject to four week rule)	22
Interviewed in full	18
Refused	1
Failed to keep appointments	3

List of interviewing areas
(The regional groupings are those designated by DHSS with the exception of Inner London).

North West
Blackpool

West Midlands
Stoke North
Birmingham North West
Birmingham South
Wolverhampton North
Dudley

South West
Bath
Weston-super-Mare
Newton Abbot
Swindon

London South (excluding Inner London)
  Worthing
  Crawley
  Kingston
  Morden
  Redhill
  Surbiton

London West (excluding Inner London)
  High Wycombe
  Newport Pagnell
  Slough
  Fareham
  Bournemouth

Inner London
  St Pancras
  Islington
  Havering
  St Marylebone

The questionnaire

The questionnaire for the full interview with those who had been subjected to the four week rule was semi-structured. The questions were carefully phrased and, where appropriate, precoded answer categories were provided; but in many cases the answers were recorded verbatim and interviewers were instructed to probe fully to obtain as much information as possible. They encouraged the respondent to talk freely, to express his attitudes and to describe any special circumstances or problems in detail. The interview therefore required more skill and judgement on the part of the interviewer than the average fully structured questionnaire. All the interviewers were personally briefed in a half day briefing session which included a detailed trial interview. The interviews took between forty-five minutes and one-and-a-half-hours depending on frequency and length of unemployment.

Copies of the questionnaire are available from the author,

together with the contact questionnaire which was used to establish whether a single man under forty-five was eligible for interview. Both were piloted during the feasibility study and revised before the main survey.